Taxcafe Tax Guides

Pension Magic

How to Make the Taxman Pay for Your Retirement

By Nick Braun PhD

Important Legal Notices:

Published by:
Taxcafe UK Limited
67 Milton Road
Kirkcaldy KY1 1TL
Tel: (0044) 01592 560081
Email: team@taxcafe.co.uk

10th Edition, May 2020

ISBN 978-1-911020-55-4

Disclaimer
Before reading or relying on the content of this tax guide please read the disclaimer.

TAX Cafe®

Pay Less Tax!

with help from Taxcafe's unique tax guides

All products available online at

www.taxcafe.co.uk

Popular Taxcafe titles include:

How to Save Property Tax

Using a Property Company to Save Tax

How to Save Inheritance Tax

The Big Landlord Tax Increase

Salary versus Dividends

Using a Company to Save Tax

Small Business Tax Saving Tactics

Keeping it Simple:
Small Business Bookkeeping, Tax & VAT

Tax Planning for Non-Residents & Non Doms

Pension Magic

How to Save Tax

Disclaimer

1. This guide is intended as **general guidance** only and does NOT constitute accountancy, tax, financial, investment or other professional advice.

2. The author and Taxcafe UK Limited make no representations or warranties with respect to the accuracy or completeness of this publication and cannot accept any responsibility or liability for any loss or risk, personal or otherwise, which may arise, directly or indirectly, from reliance on information contained in this publication.

3. Please note that tax legislation, the law and practices by Government and regulatory authorities (e.g. HM Revenue & Customs) are constantly changing. We therefore recommend that for accountancy, tax, financial, investment or other professional advice, you consult a suitably qualified accountant, tax advisor, financial adviser, or other professional adviser.

4. Please also note that your personal circumstances may vary from the general examples given in this guide and your professional adviser will be able to give specific advice based on your personal circumstances.

5. This guide covers UK taxation only and any references to 'tax' or 'taxation', unless the contrary is expressly stated, refer to UK taxation only. Please note that references to the 'UK' do not include the Channel Islands or the Isle of Man. Foreign tax implications are beyond the scope of this guide.

6. All persons described in the examples in this guide are entirely fictional. Any similarities to actual persons, living or dead, or to fictional characters created by any other author, are entirely coincidental.

Dedication

Once again, to Aileen for all your love and support and to Jake, Sandy and Tilly for all the joy you bring.

About the Author & Taxcafe

Dr Nick Braun founded Taxcafe in 1999, along with his partner Aileen Smith. As the driving force behind the company, their aim is to provide affordable plain-English tax information for private individuals, business owners and professional advisors.

Over the past 20 years Taxcafe has become one of the best-known tax publishers in the UK and has won several prestigious business awards.

Nick has been a specialist tax writer since 1989, first in South Africa, where he edited the monthly *Tax Breaks* publication, and since 1999 in the UK, where he has authored several tax books including *Small Business Tax Saving Tactics* and *Salary versus Dividends*.

Nick also has a PhD in economics from the University of Glasgow, where he was awarded the prestigious William Glen scholarship and later became a Research Fellow.

Contents

Introduction

Let's get straight down to business. There is only one reason why you should put money into a pension and that is to SAVE TAX.

As a pension saver you enjoy two important tax reliefs:

- Tax relief on your contributions – what I call buying investments at a 40% discount.

- Tax-free growth – all your income and capital gains are completely tax free.

However, if maximising tax relief is your priority, as it should be, there's a lot more to it than simply putting away a fixed amount each year.

You may wish to decide *how much* to invest, making bigger or smaller pension contributions in some years or none at all.

You may wish to consider *who* makes the contributions: you, your employer, or your spouse.

You may also want to look at *when* is the best time to invest.

And, of course, you may want to know *why* you should even bother investing in a pension in the first place. For example, are pensions better than other investments like ISAs and Lifetime ISAs?

All of these important issues are addressed in this guide and I think you will be surprised by some of the results.

In Part 1 we explain how tax relief on pension contributions is calculated and how much you are allowed to invest. However, as we shall discover, calculating the maximum pension contribution you *can* make is not as important as calculating the maximum pension contribution you *should* make to maximise your tax relief.

Over 200,000 people do not claim all the tax relief to which they are entitled, so we also explain how you can make a backdated tax relief claim and avoid other common mistakes that could cost you thousands of pounds.

Pension Freedom Has Arrived

Up until recently the amount of money you could withdraw from your pension was tightly controlled. Most individuals' savings could only come out at a trickle, either through one of those universally detested annuities or something called "capped drawdown".

These restrictions have now been lifted completely, giving pension savers more control over their money than they have ever had.

Once you reach the minimum retirement age (currently 55) you have complete freedom to withdraw as much or as little money as you like from your pension pot, whenever you like.

For the first time, pension savers have the ability to control their tax bills, by making big pension withdrawals in some tax years and smaller withdrawals in others.

The Government has also removed another of the major obstacles that has put people off using pensions to save for retirement. Up until recently, when you died your remaining pension savings were taxed at 55% before being passed on to certain family members.

This hefty tax charge has now been abolished and pension pots can be inherited by family members with no adverse tax penalties.

In Part 2 of the guide we explain all of the "Pension Freedom" changes and show you how to save thousands of pounds in both income tax and capital gains tax by timing your pension withdrawals carefully.

In Part 3 we show how pensions are much more powerful tax shelters than ISAs. We track two investors over a number of years and reveal that a pension saver could end up with 41.67% more retirement income than an ISA investor.

We also explain some of the lesser known tax differences between ISAs and pensions (for example, why some dividend income is taxed inside an ISA and why your family may be better off if your money is in a pension).

Postponing & Accelerating Pension Contributions

Those under the age of 40 can now open a "Lifetime ISA" and use it to save either for a first home or for retirement.

In Part 3 we'll tell you everything you need to know about this fantastic new saving vehicle and why some taxpayers will end up with 18% more retirement income if they use a Lifetime ISA instead of a traditional pension.

In Part 4 we look at the pros and cons of postponing and accelerating pension contributions. We show how basic-rate taxpayers – those earning under £50,000 – can increase their pension pots by 33% by delaying making pension contributions for several years.

This part of the guide also contains a fascinating case study which reveals that even if you postpone pension contributions for several years you will not necessarily end up one penny worse off than someone who makes pension contributions for many years.

There is one group who should always consider making pension contributions: households where the highest earner's income is between £50,000 and £60,000 and child benefit is being claimed. Your family's child benefit payments are steadily taken away as your income rises from £50,000 to £60,000. By using pension contributions to reduce taxable income, people in this income bracket can enjoy tax relief of up to 73% or more!

Employees, Business Owners & Landlords

In Parts 5 to 8 we look at different types of pension saver: salaried employees, company owners, self-employed business owners and landlords.

In Part 5 we explain 'auto-enrolment': the compulsory pensions that have resulted in many employees enjoying a pension contribution from their employer for the first time.

Some individuals who can receive free money from their employers in the shape of a company pension contribution may decide not to take up the offer. So in this part of the guide we also publish an interesting table which shows you just how much bigger your pension pot will be if you take full advantage of the free cash your employer is offering.

Part 6 looks at salary sacrifice pensions, which can boost your pension contributions by an astonishing 34%. Salary sacrifice pensions allow you to claw back not just income tax but *national insurance* as well, including the 13.8% national insurance paid by your employer.

A salary sacrifice pension is not just a tax-efficient way to save for retirement, it is arguably the most powerful tax-saving tool available to salaried employees.

Part 7 covers company owners and directors and reveals why company pension contributions are a highly tax-efficient way to extract money from your business. We also explain why getting your company to make the pension contributions is currently more tax efficient than making the contributions yourself.

There is also a chapter looking at the benefits and drawbacks of using your pension to make a loan to your company – you can do this if you have a small self-administered pension scheme (SSAS).

Most of this guide is relevant to self-employed business owners (sole traders and the like). Some additional practical pointers are provided in Part 8 to help this group maximise their tax relief.

I've also included a chapter for landlords. It explains how, with the help of pension contributions, you can reverse the tax increase you may suffer now that your buy-to-let mortgage interest is no longer fully tax deductible. The final chapter in Part 8 looks at the pros and cons of putting commercial property into a pension.

Part 9 answers a key family pension planning question: "Who should make the pension contributions, me or my spouse/partner?" There is also a chapter looking at the pros and cons of opening a pension for your children or grandchildren.

Pension Planning and the Coronavirus Crisis

Part 10 is a brand new section which explains how the coronavirus crisis affects pensions and retirement planning.

There's a chapter that tells you all the pros and cons of withdrawing money from your pension pot if you need cash now, before you retire.

You will also find out how fraudsters promise to "unlock" your pension before age 55 and try to persuade people to transfer their retirement savings into bogus pension schemes.

The biggest chapter in this part of the guide looks at why some people should consider reducing or postponing their pension contributions if they are worried about their finances at present.

There are two reasons why you may wish to consider postponing your pension contributions for a while.

One is so that you can protect your finances and build up some cash to help tide you through any economic downturn caused by the coronavirus crisis.

We will see that it is possible to make catch-up contributions in the future without causing any damage to your retirement plans.

The second reason you may wish to postpone your pension contributions is to maximise your higher-rate tax relief. If your income falls this year because of the coronavirus crisis, you may not enjoy any or as much higher-rate tax relief. However, if you postpone some or all of your pension contributions you may be able to double your tax relief.

Another chapter in this new section looks at possible future tax increases that may affect how much tax relief you will receive on your pension contributions in the years ahead.

The final chapter takes a brief looks at all of the other tax shelters and why you should or should not keep using them in the current climate.

I hope you find *Pension Magic* an enjoyable and interesting read.

Scope of this Guide

This guide does not cover every aspect of pension saving. The focus is *maximising tax relief*, which is the main reason people invest in the first place.

I do not cover issues like pension charges, how you should invest your money (in shares, funds, bonds, property etc), or how to choose a pension provider. I make no excuses for these omissions. As it is I've struggled to keep the guide to around 265 pages, focusing almost entirely on tax saving strategies.

Furthermore, the focus of this guide is defined contribution pension schemes, also known as money purchase schemes. These include all individual pensions (for example, personal pensions and SIPPs) and most company pension schemes these days. The basic idea is you (and your employer if you have one) put money in and the amount of income you get out at the end of the day depends on how well your investments have performed.

There is very little discussion of defined benefit or final salary pension schemes. With this type of scheme your employer promises to pay you a pension based on your salary and years of service. Final salary schemes are increasingly scarce in the private sector because employers are unwilling to guarantee to pay someone a set amount of income for the rest of their life. However, they are still the order of the day in the public sector, with the taxpayer forced to pick up the tab.

Scottish Taxpayers

Pensions are all about income tax and income tax in Scotland is different to the rest of the UK. Most of the information in this guide is relevant to Scottish taxpayers. However, unless stated to the contrary, all examples and calculations are based on the assumption that the taxpayer concerned is not a Scottish taxpayer.

Finally, please remember that this guide is not meant to be a substitute for proper professional advice. Before you act you should contact either a suitably qualified accountant, tax advisor, IFA or pensions expert who understands your personal circumstances.

Part 1

Putting Money In:
The Pension Contribution Rules

Chapter 1

Tax Relief on Contributions: How it's Calculated

When you make pension contributions the taxman will top up your savings by paying cash directly into your plan. Effectively for every £80 you invest, the taxman will put in an extra £20.

Why £20, you might be asking? Well your contributions are treated as having been paid out of income that has already been taxed at the basic income tax rate of 20%. The taxman is therefore refunding the income tax you've already paid.

The company that manages your pension plan – usually an insurance company or SIPP provider – will claim this money for you from the taxman and credit it to your account.

So whatever contribution you make personally, divide it by 0.80 and you'll get the total amount that is invested in your pension pot.

Example
Peter invests £4,000 in a self-invested personal pension (SIPP). After the taxman makes his top-up payment, the total amount of money Peter will have sitting in his pension pot is £5,000:

$$£4,000/0.80 = £5,000$$

Basic-rate tax relief isn't the end of the story. If Peter is a *higher-rate* taxpayer, paying tax at 40%, he'll be able to claim even more tax relief.

The Cherry on Top – Higher Rate Relief

For the 2020/21 tax year a higher-rate taxpayer is someone who earns more than £50,000.

If you are a higher-rate taxpayer the taxman will let you claim your higher-rate tax relief when you submit your tax return.

Alternatively, if you are a company employee, higher-rate tax relief can be provided immediately by reducing the tax paid on your salary via your PAYE code.

(See Chapter 5 for more information on how to claim higher-rate tax relief.)

Example
As we already know, Peter's personal contribution is £4,000 and total pension fund investment, including the taxman's top-up, is:

$$£4,000/0.80 = £5,000$$

The £4,000 is what's known as the 'net contribution' and the £5,000 is what's known as the 'gross contribution'.

Multiplying the gross contribution by 20% we get:

$$£5,000 \times 20\% = £1,000$$

This is Peter's higher-rate tax relief.

Effectively he has a pension investment of £5,000 which has cost him just £3,000 (£4,000 personal contribution less his £1,000 tax refund). In other words, he is getting all of his investments at a 40% discount.

This is the critical number. Being able to make investments year after year at a 40% discount can have a huge effect on the amount of wealth you accumulate.

Scottish Taxpayers 2020/21

The Scottish Parliament now has the power to set income tax rates and thresholds for most types of income, most notably salaries, self-employment income, rental income and pensions. Interest and dividend income are still taxed using UK rates and thresholds.

Income tax in Scotland is being levied as follows in 2020/21:

£0 - £12,500	0%	Personal allowance
£12,500 - £14,585	19%	Starter rate
£14,585 - £25,158	20%	Basic rate
£25,158 - £43,430	21%	Intermediate rate
£43,430 - £150,000	41%	Higher rate
£150,000 +	46%	Top rate

Scottish taxpayers who pay tax at just 19%, or pay no tax at all, will continue to enjoy 20% tax relief on their pension contributions.

Those who pay the 21% intermediate rate can claim the additional 1% tax relief by getting HMRC to adjust their tax code, completing a tax return or contacting HMRC. The same goes for those paying 41% tax or 46% tax.

Summary

- When you make pension contributions you qualify for two types of tax relief: Basic-rate tax relief which comes in the shape of top-ups to your pension plan and higher-rate relief which is normally claimed when you submit your tax return.

- Your total pension fund investment is found by dividing your personal contribution by 0.80. The taxman's top-up is paid directly to your pension provider who will credit your pension pot.

- Higher-rate relief is calculated by multiplying your gross pension fund contribution by 20%.

- Together these two tax reliefs mean all your pension investments come in at a 40% discount.

Chapter 2

How Much Can You Invest?

In this chapter we will examine the rules that determine how much you can invest in a pension each year.

Note that successive governments have continually tampered with the pension system, for better or worse. If you are making pension contributions over several decades you should not rely on the same set of rules applying in 5, 10 or 20 years' time.

The good news, for now at least, is that it's possible for most individuals to make big enough pension contributions and enjoy full income tax relief.

Age

This is a good one to kick off with. Generally anyone up to the ripe old age of 75 can make pension contributions.

In the March 2014 Budget the Government announced that it would explore whether this age limit should be changed or abolished. Following consultation, it was decided not to make any changes, so the age limit remains at 75.

There is effectively no lower age limit. You may not be able to set up your own pension plan if you're under 18 years of age but some pension providers have special products so that parents and grandparents can make pension contributions for their children and grandchildren (see Chapter 39 for more information).

Multiple Pension Schemes

Up until a few years ago many members of workplace schemes could not contribute to a second pension, such as a self-invested personal pension (SIPP). This is no longer the case.

Most people can now contribute to more than one pension and have more control over how their retirement savings are invested.

The Basic Pension Contribution Rule

To obtain tax relief on your pension contributions they have to stay within certain limits:

- **Earnings**. Contributions made by you *personally* must not exceed your annual earnings.

- **The £40,000 Annual Allowance.** Total pension contributions by you and anyone else (normally your employer) must not exceed £40,000 per year. The annual allowance is reduced once you start withdrawing certain types of income from your pension (see below). It may also be reduced if your "adjusted income" exceeds £240,000 (see Chapter 20 for more details).

Ignoring any pension contributions by the employer, an individual with earnings of £35,000 can contribute £35,000 to a pension. An individual with earnings of £75,000 can contribute £40,000 (contributions capped by the annual allowance).

Employer contributions also have to be thrown into the mix when calculating the maximum pension contribution.

Let's say the individual with earnings of £75,000 is an employee and his employer contributes £10,000 to his pension. The maximum contribution he can make personally is £30,000:

£40,000 annual allowance – £10,000 from employer = £30,000

How Relevant Is this to Me?

Almost everyone making pension contributions needs to understand what is meant by the term 'earnings'. Earnings are not the same as income.

The annual allowance, on the other hand, does not affect most people because most of us do not have anything close to £40,000 paid into our pension plans each year. However, as we shall see in Part 4, there may be times when you want to make big catch-up contributions. In these circumstances it is important to know a bit more about how the annual allowance operates.

Gross vs Cash Contributions

The above pension contribution limits are for *gross* pension contributions. However, the money you actually pay into your pension is normally NOT a gross pension contribution (unless you belong to certain types of occupational pension scheme). To calculate your gross contributions you have to add on basic-rate tax relief (the taxman's top up). You do that by dividing your actual cash contribution by 0.80.

How does this affect the pension contribution limits? If you have earnings of £35,000 you cannot pay £35,000 into your pension plan. You can only pay in £28,000 (£35,000 x 0.8). The taxman will add a further £7,000 in tax relief, bringing your total gross pension contribution to £35,000.

Similarly, the £40,000 annual allowance is a cap on total gross pension contributions. So the maximum cash pension contribution an individual can make in the absence of any employer contributions is £32,000 (£40,000 x 0.8), with the taxman adding a further £8,000 in tax relief.

Employer Contributions

Contributions by employers are always gross contributions. When your employer puts money into your pension plan there is no additional top up from the taxman. Instead the company obtains tax relief by claiming employee pension contributions as a tax deductible business expense.

So if your employer contributes £10,000 to your pension that will be a gross contribution and the maximum gross contribution you can make personally is £30,000:

$$£40,000 - £10,000 = £30,000$$

The maximum amount you can actually pay into your pension plan would then be £24,000:

$$£30,000 \times 0.8 = £24,000$$

You can only make this maximum contribution if you have earnings of at least £30,000.

14

Occupational Pension Schemes

For many employees who belong to occupational schemes, the actual pension contribution is the same as the gross pension contribution.

Under the 'net pay arrangement' the employer deducts the employee's pension contributions from the employee's gross pay *before* tax is deducted. This means full tax relief is obtained immediately by paying the contribution out of pre-tax income. There is no top up by the taxman and no need to claim higher-rate tax relief via a tax return.

(Similarly, Scottish employees who now pay tax at 21% or more do not have to claim back their additional tax relief from HMRC if they belong to a net pay arrangement – see previous chapter.)

Not all contributions by employees are made gross. If the employer has a pension scheme that uses 'relief at source' (usually group personal pensions), the employee's contributions are paid after the employee's salary has been taxed. Basic-rate relief is then claimed by the pension scheme and added to the member's pension pot to obtain their total gross pension contribution.

Earnings

To obtain tax relief on your pension contributions you have to have earnings – 'relevant UK earnings' to be precise.

Employees

If you are an employee, your relevant UK earnings will include:

- Salary or wages
- Bonus, overtime, and commissions, and
- Taxable benefits in kind.

There are a few other bits and bobs that can count as relevant UK earnings for pension contribution purposes, including redundancy payments that exceed the £30,000 tax-free threshold and statutory sick pay and statutory maternity pay.

Company Directors

Most small company owners are also directors. For pension contribution purposes company directors are treated just like regular employees. Their relevant UK earnings include their salary, bonus, overtime, commissions and taxable benefits in kind.

As shareholders of their companies they can also pay themselves dividends. To save tax and national insurance, many company owners take a small tax-free salary and take the rest of their income as dividends.

It is often tax efficient for company owners to pay themselves a salary equal to the national insurance threshold (£9,500 for 2020/21) and take the rest of their income as dividends (see Chapter 31).

The problem, however, is that dividends are NOT earnings. As such, a company director with a salary of £9,500 and dividends of £50,000 can only contribute £9,500 to a pension.

The actual cash contribution would be £7,600 (£9,500 x 0.8) with the taxman adding £1,900 in tax relief for a gross contribution of £9,500.

Fortunately for company owners, they can get their companies to make pension contributions (employer contributions) and these are not restricted to their earnings (although they are restricted by the £40,000 annual allowance). We'll take a closer look at pension planning for company owners in Part 7.

The Self-Employed

Most people would regard any business owner as 'self-employed'. However, when HMRC talks about 'self-employed' individuals they are referring specifically to owners of unincorporated businesses, in other words businesses that are not companies.

The most common are sole traders (one-person businesses) and partnerships.

If you are a sole trader your relevant UK earnings are generally the pre-tax profits of the business. If you are a partner, your relevant UK earnings will be your share of the partnership's pre-tax profit.

The problem is that many self-employed individuals don't know what their pre-tax profits are!

Many have an accounting period that is the same as the tax year, running to 5 April each year or 31 March. This can create a practical problem when it comes to maximising tax relief on pension contributions.

Although most salary earners (including company directors) have earnings that are fairly predictable (their salaries), the exact profits on which self-employed business owners can base their pension contributions may not be known until the accounts are drawn up *after* the tax year has ended.

In other words, as a self-employed business owner you may only know what your relevant UK earnings are when it is too late to make pension contributions. You cannot make back-dated pension contributions after the tax year has ended. I'll explain how this practical problem can be fixed in Chapter 35.

Income but Not Earnings

Earnings do not include:

- Rental income
- Interest
- Dividends
- Capital gains

For example, if you have earnings of £30,000 and rental income of £20,000 from buy-to-let properties, the maximum gross pension contribution you can make is £30,000.

With regards to rental income, there is one exception. When it comes to tax, owners of furnished holiday lettings are treated quite differently to other rental property owners and pensions are no exception. Profits from furnished holiday lettings count as relevant UK earnings for pension purposes.

Individuals with No Earnings

Some people don't have any earnings, including non-working spouses and minor children.

Many professional landlords, who derive all of their income from rental properties, will also not have any earnings.

The good news is that everyone under the age of 75 can make a pension contribution of £3,600 per year, regardless of earnings. The actual cash contribution would be £2,880, with the taxman adding £720 to bring the total gross contribution to £3,600.

We'll take a closer look at the pros and cons of making pension contributions when you have no earnings in Part 9.

The Annual Allowance

The annual allowance is the overall cap on the amount of pension contributions you can make with tax relief. It's currently £40,000.

Your annual allowance is reduced once you start withdrawing certain types of income from your pension (see below).

Your annual allowance is also reduced if your "adjusted income" exceeds £240,000 (see Chapter 20 for more details).

The annual allowance includes pension contributions made by both you and anyone else (normally your employer).

If your contributions do exceed the annual allowance, you can carry forward unused allowance from the three previous tax years.

If the annual allowance is exceeded, and the excess is not covered by carry forward, the excess is taxed at your marginal income tax rate (20%, 40% or 45%).

This annual allowance charge can be paid when you submit your tax return or deducted from your pension savings if it's over £2,000.

In practice, the annual allowance is generous enough for most people and very few will be affected by it. Those who have to be most careful are those making big one-off pension contributions.

Another group that has to be careful are members of final salary pension schemes (also known as defined benefit pension schemes).

The value of their pension benefits can increase by significantly more than £40,000 in the year they receive a substantial pay increase. Professional advice should also be obtained in these circumstances.

Pension Input Periods

Up until recently, when calculating whether the annual allowance was exceeded, you didn't count pension contributions made during a *tax year* (5 April to 6 April). Instead you used the pension scheme's annual *pension input period*.

As a result, quite big pension contributions made during two different tax years could have fallen into just one pension input period and exceeded the annual allowance.

However, with effect from 6 April 2016 all pension input periods are now aligned with the tax year.

The Carry Forward Rule

If you want to make a big pension contribution that exceeds the annual allowance you can tap any unused allowance from the three previous tax years.

This means that someone who hasn't made any pension contributions so far during the current tax year can potentially make a pension contribution of up to £160,000 in 2020/21 and enjoy full tax relief:

- £40,000 for 2020/21
- £40,000 for 2019/20
- £40,000 for 2018/19
- £40,000 for 2017/18

Example

Paula is a sole trader and makes bumper profits of £150,000 during the 2020/21 tax year.

She transfers £80,000 into her pension plan, resulting in a gross pension contribution of £100,000 (£80,000/0.8).

Her gross pension contributions in the three previous tax years were:

	Pension Contribution	Unused Annual Allowance
2019/20	£20,000	£20,000
2018/19	£20,000	£20,000
2017/18	£10,000	£30,000

In total Paula has £70,000 of unused annual allowance.

Together with the £40,000 annual allowance for the current tax year, Paula can make a total gross pension contribution of up to £110,000.

Her £100,000 gross pension contribution is therefore within the limits and does not exceed her earnings and therefore enjoys full tax relief.

You use the annual allowance for the current tax year first. You then use your unused annual allowance from the *earliest* tax year first (2017/18 in Paula's case).

This leaves any unused allowance from the most recent tax years free to be carried forward.

In Paula's case she will be able to carry forward £10,000 of unused allowance from 2019/20 and use it in a future tax year.

Earnings Can't Be Carried Forward

The pension contributions you make personally cannot exceed your earnings for the current tax year.

Although you can carry forward unused annual allowance, you cannot carry forward earnings from previous years or make backdated pension contributions.

Membership of a Pension Scheme Required

Unused annual allowance can only be carried forward if you were a member of a registered pension scheme for the period in question.

For example, if you start contributing to a pension now but did not belong to any pension scheme in the three previous tax years, you cannot carry forward any unused annual allowance from those years.

On a practical level, this means that someone who does not currently have a pension plan in place, but may wish to make big contributions in a few years' time, should consider setting one up as soon as possible.

Getting your Contribution Right

The pension contribution rules are quite complex... but only if you have quite big contributions and are in danger of exceeding the annual allowance.

Most people will not have anything close to £40,000 per year added to their pension pots and are completely unaffected by the annual allowance rules (individuals who want to make big catch-up contributions are an important exception – see Chapter 18).

The earnings limit is also irrelevant for the vast majority of people. Most would never contemplate contributing anything close to 100% of their earnings to a pension. (Company directors are one exception because they often pay themselves a small tax-free salary and therefore have very low 'earnings'.)

I don't want to sound flippant but it's important not to become bogged down by rules that may never affect you. Calculating the maximum pension contribution you *can* make is not the important issue for most people. What is far more important is calculating the maximum pension contribution you *should* make.

A far more important calculation for many individuals is the maximum contribution that will obtain full higher-rate tax relief. This is the subject of Chapter 4.

Contributions after Withdrawals Have Started

When you start withdrawing income from your pension your ability to make further pension contributions could be severely restricted.

You may no longer be entitled to a £40,000 annual allowance. Instead your contributions could be subject to the 'money purchase annual allowance'.

The money purchase annual allowance is now just £4,000. It was reduced from £10,000 to £4,000 on 6 April 2017.

There are other anti-avoidance rules designed to prevent money being taken out of a pension in order to make new pension contributions, thereby benefiting from two rounds of tax relief.

If you use your tax-free lump sum to significantly increase your pension contributions, the contributions may fall foul of HMRC's recycling rules and a tax charge of up to 70% could be imposed.

We'll take a closer look at both these issues in Part 2 which deals with taking money out of pensions.

Chapter 3

The Lifetime Allowance

The lifetime allowance is the maximum amount of money you are allowed to save up in pensions with full tax relief.

It was reduced from £1.8 million to £1.5 million in 2012 and to £1.25 million in 2014. In 2016 it was reduced again to £1 million.

The Government then promised to increase the lifetime allowance in line with inflation. It has been increased to £1,073,100 for the current 2020/21 tax year.

It's impossible to predict what will happen to inflation in the years ahead but if it averages 2% per year then by 2028 the lifetime allowance will be back up to around £1,250,000.

Of course, there's nothing to stop the current or any future government reversing course and reducing the allowance again!

If your pension savings exceed the lifetime allowance you will have to pay the lifetime allowance charge on the excess.

The lifetime allowance charge is 55% if the excess funds are paid out as a lump sum (this is only possible before age 75). The tax charge is 25% if the excess funds are retained inside the pension plan, with income tax also payable on any withdrawals.

Basic-rate taxpayers will usually be better off withdrawing the excess funds as taxable income because the overall tax rate will be 40% instead of 55%. Higher-rate taxpayers will pay roughly the same amount of tax on excess lump sums and income. However, paying the 25% charge may be preferable so that the money can continue to grow tax free inside the pension plan and stay outside the inheritance tax net (see Chapter 10).

In this chapter I will not spend too much time explaining how the lifetime allowance charge is applied in practice if your pension savings go over the limit. Instead I will try to answer the more important questions: Are my pension savings likely to exceed the lifetime allowance? If so, does it really matter?

How is the Lifetime Allowance Applied?

Your pension savings will be tested against the lifetime allowance when there is a "benefit crystallisation event" – typically when you start withdrawing money, even if it's just your tax-free lump sum.

The lifetime allowance test also takes place if you reach age 75 with pension savings that haven't been touched yet.

If you place your pension into drawdown when you retire you may face a second lifetime allowance test when you reach age 75.

(You may also face this second lifetime allowance test if you use your drawdown funds to later buy an annuity.)

This second test may affect you if your drawdown fund has grown in size, for example if you've continued working and haven't withdrawn much money from it or have enjoyed very high investment returns.

But if your drawdown fund has fallen in value (for example, if you've been withdrawing money steadily) there will be nothing additional to measure against the lifetime allowance.

Example

Saul is 65 and has a pension fund worth £800,000. In 2020/21 he takes a tax-free lump sum of £200,000 and moves the remaining £600,000 into drawdown. The lifetime allowance is £1,073,100 in 2020/21 so Saul does not have to pay the lifetime allowance charge. With an £800,000 pension pot this benefit crystallisation event uses up 75% of his lifetime allowance, leaving him with 25% for future use.

He keeps working and doesn't withdraw any income from his drawdown fund. 10 years later his drawdown fund has grown from £600,000 to £1 million. Because he's now 75 there's a second lifetime allowance test. The amount crystallised is the current value of his drawdown fund less its original value: £1 million - £600,000 = £400,000.

Let's assume that when Saul is 75 the lifetime allowance has increased with inflation to £1.3 million. Saul is entitled to 25% of this, i.e. £325,000. Thus Saul will face a lifetime allowance charge on £75,000 (£400,000 - £325,000). The excess funds are subject to a lifetime allowance charge of 25% (£18,750) and he can withdraw the rest as taxable income.

It should be fairly easy for Saul to avoid the lifetime allowance charge altogether by simply withdrawing enough money before he is 75. He should withdraw the amount his drawdown fund has grown over and above his remaining lifetime allowance.

Because the withdrawals will be subject to income tax he may be better off doing this over several tax years to avoid paying tax at 40% or more.

Am I in Danger of Exceeding the Lifetime Allowance?

Arguably those most at risk of going over the lifetime allowance are long-serving members of final salary pension schemes. The annual pension you receive is generally multiplied by 20 and added to any additional lump sum you receive.

For example, with a lifetime allowance of £1,073,100, someone retiring with a final salary pension of more than £53,655 per year (with no separate lump sum) could be subject to the lifetime allowance charge (£53,655 x 20 = £1,073,100).

It's also possible that some members of modern occupational pension schemes in the private sector and those with SIPPs and personal pensions will breach the lifetime allowance.

Members of these "money purchase" pension schemes could end up paying the lifetime allowance charge if they have made successful investments, saved hard or received generous contributions from their employers.

However, it's vital to stress that the vast majority of people are in danger of saving too little, not too much, in pensions.

Table 1 will give you some idea whether you're in danger of exceeding the lifetime allowance.

The table shows how many years it will take your existing pension pot and annual contributions to exceed the lifetime allowance.

Table 1
Number of Years until
Lifetime Allowance Exceeded

Annual Gross Pension Contribution

Current Pot	£0k	£5k	£10k	£15k	£20k	£25k	£30	£35k	£40k
£0k	n/a	47	36	29	25	22	20	19	18
£100k	45	34	28	24	21	19	17	16	15
£150k	37	29	25	21	19	17	16	14	14
£200k	32	26	22	19	17	16	14	13	13
£250k	28	23	20	18	16	14	13	12	12
£300k	24	20	18	16	14	13	12	11	11
£400k	19	16	14	13	12	11	10	9	9
£500k	14	13	11	10	9	9	8	8	7
£600k	12	10	9	8	7	7	6	6	6
£700k	8	7	7	6	6	5	5	5	4
£800k	5	5	5	4	4	4	3	3	3
£900k	3	3	3	3	2	2	2	2	2
£1m	1	1	1	1	1	1	1	1	1

Example

Ann is 50, has pension savings of £100,000 and is making an annual pension contribution of £10,000. The table tells us her pension pot will exceed the lifetime allowance in 28 years' time.

Ann intends to stop working and start withdrawing money from her pension in just 10 years' time, when she is 60. So the lifetime allowance does not pose any risk to her.

A much more relevant question is: Will Ann's pension pot be big enough to retire on? In 10 years' time she will have pension savings of roughly £370,000 which seems a bit on the low side to me, unless she has a spouse or partner who also has pension savings.

(Note, if you reach age 75 with uncrystallised (untouched) pension savings, those savings will be tested against the lifetime allowance at age 75. So in practice the maximum amount of time before Ann's pension pot will be tested is 25 years, not 28 years.)

Table 1 Assumptions

The figures in Table 1 were calculated by making the following assumptions:

- The lifetime allowance increases by 2% per year (the assumed rate of inflation). Remember, a future government could freeze or reduce the lifetime allowance

- Annual pension contributions also increase by 2% per year

- Once annual contributions reach £40,000 (the level of the annual allowance) there are no further increases

- The annual allowance is not affected by the restriction for those with over £240,000 adjusted income (see Chapter 20)

- Annual pension contributions include contributions by both the individual and any employer and also include basic-rate tax relief (the taxman's top up)

- Pension investments grow by 7.5% per year. With 2% inflation this equates to a real return of roughly 5.5% per year which is roughly what the UK stock market has delivered since 1900

It should be stressed that, when doing calculations like these that cover long periods of time, the outcome can be altered dramatically by tweaking the numbers just slightly.

For example, the last assumption possibly overstates future investment returns by ignoring fees and charges. If net investment returns are lower than 7.5%, it will take longer to exceed the lifetime allowance than the table suggests.

For example, let's say you have a pension pot of £200,000 and pension contributions of £15,000 per year. Table 1 tells us that you will exceed the lifetime allowance in roughly 19 years' time.

But if your investments grow by just 5% per year it will take 27 years to exceed the lifetime allowance. And if your investments grow by 10% per year it will take just 15 years to exceed the lifetime allowance.

Some of the other assumptions could also be called into question. For example, there's a good chance your salary and therefore your pension contributions will grow faster than inflation as you climb the career ladder. If so your pension pot will exceed the lifetime allowance sooner than the table suggests.

It may also be unreasonable to assume that the annual allowance will never increase above £40,000. Surely it must go up at some point to compensate for inflation? In defence of this assumption, some politicians are still calling for the annual allowance to be cut.

Small Pension Pot, Big Catch Up Contributions

Let's say you haven't saved up much money in a pension yet and want to make big catch up contributions.

The table tells us that someone who doesn't have one penny of pension savings and saves the maximum amount of £40,000 per year will exceed the lifetime allowance after just 18 years.

This won't be a problem if the individual is getting closer to retirement and wants to start withdrawing money within the next 18 years (for example, those in their late forties or older).

It may be a problem if you are younger. For example, if you are 35 your pension savings will exceed the lifetime allowance by the time you are 53. By the time you reach the minimum retirement age (probably 57 – see Chapter 7), there's a good chance your pension savings will be well in excess of the lifetime allowance.

Big Pension Pot, No More Pension Contributions

The first column of Table 1 shows how long it will take to exceed the lifetime allowance even if you stop making pension contributions.

For example, someone who currently has a £400,000 pension pot and stops making contributions will exceed the lifetime allowance in 19 years' time.

This may not be a problem if you are in your forties or older but it may be a problem if you are in your thirties.

Postponing the Lifetime Allowance Charge

It is possible to postpone the lifetime allowance charge by crystallising just enough of your pension savings to remain within the lifetime allowance.

For example, let's say when you reach the minimum retirement age you have a pension pot of £2 million and the lifetime allowance is £1.5 million. You decide to crystallise £1.5 million by taking a tax-free lump sum of £375,000 and moving the remaining £1,125,000 into drawdown where it can continue to grow tax free.

Because the amount crystallised does not exceed the lifetime allowance, no lifetime allowance charge will be payable. The remaining £500,000 will continue to grow tax free until further benefits are taken (or you reach age 75). At this point the lifetime allowance charge will be payable.

How Bad Is the Lifetime Allowance Charge?

For several years now I have argued that financial commentators spend far too much time fretting about the annual allowance and the lifetime allowance when the vast majority of people are unaffected by these restrictions.

Even if your pension savings do exceed the lifetime allowance it's not the end of the world. The charge is not as high as it first appears and your excess pension savings will still enjoy other tax benefits, including tax-free growth and protection from inheritance tax.

If you do have to pay the lifetime allowance charge you may end up no worse off than someone who puts their money in an ISA (the main alternative tax shelter).

Example
Justus invests an extra £800 in his pension and the taxman adds £200 of basic-rate tax relief, giving him a gross pension contribution of £1,000. He also receives higher-rate tax relief of £200 which means the £1,000 investment costs him just £600.

Let's also assume that Justus's friend Kevin invests £600 in an ISA – the exact same amount Justus invests (taking into account his tax relief).

Now let's look at what happens when Justus and Kevin withdraw this money. To keep the example simple we can ignore investment growth because both pensions and ISAs enjoy exactly the same tax-free growth.

However, let's assume that Justus's £1,000 pension contribution takes him over the lifetime allowance by exactly £1,000. After paying the 25% lifetime allowance charge (£250) and 20% income tax on the remaining £750 withdrawal Justus is left with £600.

Withdrawals from Kevin's ISA are tax free so he is left with £600 – exactly the same as Justus who had to pay the lifetime allowance charge.

What this example reveals is that:

Even if you have to pay the lifetime allowance charge you will end up in exactly the same position as someone who puts their money in an ISA.

In the above example I assumed that Justus is a basic-rate taxpayer when he retires. If he is a higher-rate taxpayer and pays 40% income tax on the £750 of income he withdraws he will be left with just £450.

Kevin the ISA investor will then have 33% more money than Justus the pension investor. In this case Justus would be better off putting his money in an ISA.

However, because Justus can decide how much he withdraws from his pension and when, he should be able to keep his income below the higher-rate threshold (which is currently £50,000).

Should You Try to Avoid the Charge?

Nobody wants to pay tax unnecessarily but clearly the lifetime allowance charge isn't something you should lose sleep over.

Having a pension pot worth over £1 million is something to celebrate, not mourn.

It's important not to do something harmful just to avoid the lifetime allowance charge:

- Do not opt out of your workplace pension if that means giving up pension contributions from your employer (which are effectively free money).

- Do not try to limit your investment returns to stay below the lifetime allowance, unless you want to place your pension savings into less risky investments. After all, it's better to pay 25% tax than have nothing to tax at all.

- Do not stop making pension contributions too early – it's probably better to overshoot and have a pension pot that is slightly larger than the lifetime allowance than one which is below the lifetime allowance.

Protecting Your Lifetime Allowance

If you think you may have more than £1 million of pension savings by the time you retire or reach age 75 you may wish to register for "protection".

There are two types of protection you can apply for:

- Fixed protection 2016
- Individual protection 2016

Fixed protection 2016 fixes your lifetime allowance at £1.25 million. To qualify you and your employer must not have made any pension contributions after 5 April 2016 (or have accrued benefits in a final salary scheme).

For individual protection 2016 the value of your pension savings must be more than £1 million on 5 April 2016.

It fixes your lifetime allowance at the lower of £1.25 million or the value of your pensions on 5 April 2016.

It is possible to make further pension contributions after that date.

You can apply online for both types of protection:

www.gov.uk/guidance/pension-schemes-protect-your-lifetime-allowance

There is no deadline to apply for either type of protection, although you must apply before you withdraw money from your pension.

Final Words on the Lifetime Allowance

The lifetime allowance receives a lot of press coverage and for those affected it is an important consideration.

However, the reality is that most people are in danger of saving *too little* in pensions, not too much.

Throughout this guide I therefore assume that the reader is not in any danger of breaching the lifetime allowance. If you think you may be affected, you should consider speaking to a financial advisor about your options.

Chapter 4

How to Maximise Your Higher-Rate Tax Relief

Everyone who makes pension contributions gets basic-rate tax relief (the taxman's 20% top up). If you are a higher-rate taxpayer you can also claim an additional 20% tax relief.

However, some higher-rate taxpayers don't enjoy full tax relief on their pension contributions because they don't understand how higher-rate relief is calculated.

It's a bit like paying for a business class ticket and accidentally sitting in economy.

What is a Higher-Rate Taxpayer?

A higher-rate taxpayer is currently someone who has taxable income of more than £50,000 (see below for Scottish taxpayers).

How is this number calculated? For most people the first £12,500 of income is tax free thanks to the income tax personal allowance. The next £37,500 falls into the basic-rate band and is taxed at 20%. Once your income rises above £50,000 it is taxed at 40%.

These thresholds are usually increased each year. These are the figures for the 2020/21 tax year (they were the same last year).

How Is Higher-Rate Relief Calculated?

When you make pension contributions the taxman gives you a bigger basic-rate band which means more of your income is taxed at 20% instead of 40%.

Your basic-rate band is increased by the same amount as your *gross* pension contributions.

Example

Sandy is a sole trader with pre-tax profits of £57,000. He has £7,000 of income taxed at 40% (£57,000 - £50,000).

He puts £5,000 into a pension. The taxman adds £1,250 of basic-rate relief for a gross contribution of £6,250 (£5,000/0.8).

To calculate his higher-rate relief his basic-rate band is increased by £6,250, allowing £6,250 of income to be taxed at 20% instead of 40%. This saves Sandy £1,250 in tax (£6,250 x 20%).

This is the best possible outcome. Sandy has received basic-rate and higher-rate tax relief on his entire pension contribution. In total he enjoys 40% tax relief:

$$(£1,250 + £1,250) / £6,250 = 40\%$$

The Maximum Higher Rate Relief

The maximum higher-rate tax relief you can claim is:

Your Gross Pension Contribution x 20%

However, you will only enjoy the maximum higher-rate tax relief if you have at least this much income taxed at 40%.

If your income is £50,000 plus one pound, you can only get higher-rate tax relief on one pound of pension contributions.

Sandy, whose income is £57,000, can get higher-rate tax relief on a gross pension contribution of up to £7,000 (£57,000 – £50,000). His actual gross pension contribution is £6,250 so he has stayed within the limits. If he contributes more than £7,000, the additional contribution will only get basic-rate relief.

Tax Planning

Big pension contributions can be a bad idea if you don't have enough income taxed at 40%.

To enjoy the maximum tax relief you may want to consider spreading your pension contributions over a number of tax years.

34

If maximising tax relief is your priority, you should make sure your gross pension contributions do not exceed the amount of income you have taxed at 40%.

Example revisited

Sandy is a sole trader with pre-tax profits of £57,000 in 2020/21. He has £7,000 of income taxed at 40% (£57,000 - £50,000 higher-rate threshold).

Sandy puts £15,000 into his pension. The taxman adds £3,750 of basic-rate relief. His gross contribution is £18,750 (£15,000/0.8).

His basic-rate band is increased by £18,750 which means his maximum higher-rate tax relief is:

$$£18,750 \times 20\% = £3,750$$

However, Sandy doesn't have £18,750 of income taxed at 40%, he only has £7,000. So the actual higher-rate relief he will receive is:

$$£7,000 \times 20\% = £1,400$$

Although his basic-rate band has been increased significantly, he doesn't have enough income to use it! Sandy is only obtaining higher-rate tax relief on £7,000 worth of pension contributions. In total he enjoys just 27% tax relief:

$$(£3,750 + £1,400) / £18,750 = 27\%$$

What can Sandy do if he wants to enjoy the maximum higher-rate relief? He can spread his contributions over several tax years.

If he wants to invest £15,000 (£18,750 gross) and if we assume he has £7,000 of income per year taxed at 40%, this means he could consider spreading his gross contributions over three tax years:

Year 1	£7,000
Year 2	£7,000
Year 3	£4,750

Table 2
Maximising Higher-Rate Tax Relief:
Maximum Pension Contributions 2020/21

Taxable Income £	Maximum Gross Contribution £	Maximum Cash Contribution £
50,000	0	0
55,000	5,000	4,000
60,000	10,000	8,000
65,000	15,000	12,000
70,000	20,000	16,000
75,000	25,000	20,000
80,000	30,000	24,000
85,000	35,000	28,000
90,000	40,000	32,000
95,000	45,000	36,000
100,000	50,000	40,000

Rule of Thumb

If maximising tax relief is your priority, the maximum amount you should contribute to a pension in the 2020/21 tax year is:

Your taxable income minus £50,000

This is your maximum *gross* pension contribution. Multiply this number by 0.8 to obtain the maximum amount you can actually invest (your net cash contribution).

Table 2 contains some sample maximum pension contributions for different levels of income.

Although you can contribute up to £40,000 per year to a pension (ignoring any employer contributions), only someone with income of at least £90,000 would enjoy full higher-rate tax relief on such a large gross contribution:

£90,000 - £50,000 = £40,000

Someone with income over £90,000 could contribute more than £40,000 and enjoy higher-rate tax relief on the entire contribution. However, to do this in practice they would have to carry forward unused annual allowance from previous tax years.

Big Contributions Close to Retirement

When you are close to retirement it may be worth making pension contributions that are larger than normal, even if you only enjoy basic-rate tax relief.

This is because it is possible to withdraw all the extra money you contribute immediately after you retire and 25% will be tax free.

We'll take a look at the potential tax savings in Chapter 11.

Taxpayers with Dividend Income

Some taxpayers whose *non-dividend* income is close to the higher-rate threshold (currently £50,000) may not enjoy full higher-rate relief on their pension contributions if they also have dividend income.

Example
In 2020/21 Alistair has salary and rental income of £50,000. He also has dividend income of £5,000. His dividend income all falls over the higher-rate threshold but the first £2,000 of this is tax free thanks to the dividend allowance.

If Alistair makes a gross pension contribution of £3,000 his basic-rate band will be increased by £3,000. However, we know that £2,000 of his dividend income is tax free no matter which tax band it falls into. A further £1,000 will be taxed at 7.5% instead of 32.5%, saving him £250 (25%). So Alistair's total higher-rate relief comes to £250 which is just one third the maximum relief of £750 (£3,000 x 25%).

This example will only be relevant to a small number of taxpayers. Nevertheless, what it reveals is you will not enjoy full higher-rate tax relief on your pension contributions if the first £2,000 of your dividend income falls into your increased basic-rate band.

Higher-Rate Taxpayers in Scotland

As we saw in Chapter 1, Scotland now has more income tax bands than the rest of the UK. However, the biggest increase occurs when your income rises above £43,430. At this point you become a higher-rate taxpayer and your income tax rate jumps from 21% to 41%.

So if you're a Scottish taxpayer, the maximum amount you should contribute to a pension if you want full higher-rate relief is:

Your taxable income <u>minus</u> £43,430

For example, a Scottish taxpayer who earns £50,000 can make a gross pension contribution of £6,570. This includes 20% basic-rate tax relief so the net cash contribution would be £5,256 (£6,570 x 0.8).

As a higher-rate taxpayer (paying 41% tax) an extra £1,380 of tax relief can then be claimed back (£6,570 x 21%).

Remember the Scottish Parliament can tax most types of income but NOT interest and dividends. So if you are a company owner in Scotland and pay yourself a small salary and the rest of your income comes in the shape of dividends, the relevant higher-rate threshold is the "Westminster" one – £50,000. (See Chapter 31 for more on how company directors structure their pay.)

Example
Angus is a sole trader based in Scotland with taxable income of £46,000 in 2020/21. Angus can make a gross pension contribution of £2,570 (£46,000 - £43,430) with full higher-rate tax relief.

Douglas is a company owner based in Scotland with the same amount of taxable income (£46,000) but made up mostly of dividends. If Douglas makes a pension contribution of £2,570 he will not enjoy any higher-rate tax relief because he is not a higher-rate taxpayer (the UK, not Scottish, higher-rate threshold applies to his dividend income).

Chapter 5

How to Claim
Higher-Rate Tax Relief

According to Scottish Widows, up to one quarter of higher-rate taxpayers do not claim all the tax relief they are entitled to.

Many taxpayers believe incorrectly that all of their pension tax relief is automatically credited to their pension pots.

Those who usually do NOT have to claim higher-rate tax relief are members of occupational money purchase pension schemes. Their pension contributions are paid out of their salaries before tax is deducted, so full 40% tax relief is effectively granted immediately.

Those who are affected include members of group personal pensions, group stakeholder pensions and group SIPPs. With these arrangements the contributions are made out of after-tax pay, so tax relief has to be actively claimed.

Individuals with their own private pension plans also have to actively claim their higher-rate tax relief.

Gross vs Net Contributions

Another mistake made by higher-rate taxpayers when completing tax returns is entering net cash pension contributions (the amount they actually pay in), instead of their gross contributions (which include the taxman's basic-rate tax relief top up).

Page 4 of your tax return is for 'Tax reliefs'. Box 1 asks for:

Payments to registered pension schemes where basic rate tax relief will be claimed by your pension provider (called 'relief at source'). Enter the payments and basic rate tax

If you personally pay £3,000 into your pension and insert this number on your tax return, the taxman will give you £600 of higher-rate tax relief:

$$£3,000 \times 20\% = £600$$

But if you enter the correct amount, which is £3,750 (£3,000/0.8), the taxman will give you £750 of higher-rate tax relief:

$$£3,750 \times 20\% = £750$$

Do not include employer pension contributions.

Backdated Claims

If you have not claimed your higher-rate tax relief, the good news is you can make a backdated claim going back four years. Rebates can run to thousands of pounds.

Write to your local tax office, outlining the gross contributions you have made and the tax years they relate to, or speak to an accountant.

How to Claim Higher-Rate Tax Relief

The standard way to claim higher-rate tax relief is when you submit your tax return. You can also claim it through an adjustment to your tax code. This allows tax relief to be provided immediately because less tax will be deducted from your salary each month.

(A tax code is used by your employer to calculate the amount of tax to deduct from your pay. If you have the wrong tax code you could end up paying too much tax.)

You can have your tax code adjusted by contacting HMRC and some pension companies provide template letters for this purpose.

You may need to contact HMRC again if your pension contributions increase, for example if you get a pay increase or if you make one-off contributions during the year.

Chapter 6

Higher-Rate Tax Relief:
Here to Stay?

"The gross cost of pensions tax relief is significant. Including relief on both income tax and national insurance contributions, the government forwent nearly £50 billion in 2013-14." HM Treasury

For many years now there have been fears the Government will take away the additional tax relief enjoyed by higher-rate taxpayers on their pension contributions.

Up until now this has been done *indirectly* by reducing the annual allowance from £255,000 to £40,000.

A clamp down on high earners came into effect in 2016 with the introduction of the tapered annual allowance (see Chapter 20).

Pensions – More Changes Ahead?

David Cameron's government consulted on whether to completely reform pension tax relief and an announcement was expected in the March 2016 Budget. However, in that Budget speech Chancellor George Osborne stated that "it was clear there is no consensus" and pension tax relief was left unchanged. Apparently the decision to leave pension tax relief alone was made so as not to antagonize voters ahead of the EU referendum!

A little bit later there were reports in some newspapers that George Osborne's successor, Philip Hammond, had made cutting pension tax relief a priority, following his embarrassing u-turn over national insurance for the self-employed, which left a hole in the public finances.

However, there was no mention of cutting pension tax relief in the Conservatives' 2017 election manifesto and in July 2017, while speaking to the Association of British Insurers, Secretary of State for Work and Pensions David Gauke apparently said that he did not expect to see any fundamental changes to pension tax relief in the near future.

Some in the pensions industry took comfort from this comment but then in February 2020 there was fresh speculation that former Chancellor Sajid Javid was considering cutting higher-rate tax relief. He resigned and was replaced by the current Chancellor Rishi Sunak. In his March 2020 Budget Rishi Sunak made no mention of higher-rate tax relief and instead increased the income thresholds where the tapered annual allowance applies (see Chapter 20). This allows those with high income to benefit from the £40,000 annual allowance, without any reduction.

Further changes to pension tax relief could still take place at some point in the near future, perhaps to help pay for the huge increase in Government spending during the coronavirus crisis.

And, of course, if and when there is a change of Government anything is possible. We suspect a Labour Government would treat higher-rate tax relief far less favourably than any Conservative Government.

Pensions are long-term savings vehicles, with contributions often made over many decades. It would be very brave to predict that the same level of tax relief will be available in 10 or 20 years' time.

If there is a further raid on pension tax relief it could come in the form of a further reduction in the annual allowance (from, say, £40,000 to £30,000 or £20,000) or a flat-rate model could be introduced with everyone given tax relief at say 25% or 30%. Another more radical option would be to completely replace the current pension model with something similar to the Lifetime ISA (see Chapter 14 for more on Lifetime ISAs).

The truth is nobody knows what will happen to pensions in the months and years ahead, although further changes seem likely at some point.

For several years now pension companies have advised higher-rate taxpayers to make bigger pension contributions before their extra tax relief is scrapped. To date all such predictions have been proved wrong. Nevertheless, many higher-rate taxpayers may feel they have nothing to lose by making bigger contributions with full 40% tax relief while this is still possible.

Part 2

Taking Money Out: The New Pension Freedom Rules

Chapter 7

Introduction

Before Age 55

At present you cannot withdraw any money from your pension until you're 55. This is one of the major drawbacks. There are times in life when even financially conservative individuals may need to tap their retirement savings early.

Obvious examples would be to pay for a child's education or unforeseen family medical expenses. In the worst case scenario you may even need to access your savings early to avoid bankruptcy or home repossession. So if you're under 55 and want to make significant pension contributions you should make sure you have other resources to protect against:

- Unforeseen expenses, and an
- Unforeseen drop in income.

Although you cannot withdraw anything until you're 55, it's important to point out that the money can usually be invested as you please. These days many personal pensions plans, especially SIPPs, provide enormous investment flexibility.

Note too that 55 is the minimum age set out in the legislation. The rules of a particular workplace pension scheme may impose a higher minimum age for payment of scheme benefits.

The Ill Health Exceptions

There are mainly two exceptions to the no withdrawals before age 55 rule. All pension savings can be withdrawn as a lump sum if you suffer from "serious ill health" (the polite way of saying you have less than a year to live). Withdrawals are tax free before age 75, taxable if 75 or older. You may also be able to start withdrawing money from your pension if you suffer from "ill health". This means you are not about to die but are too sick to carry on your current occupation (some scheme rules may state that you have to be incapable of carrying on *any* occupation).

Future Changes to the Pension Age

In 2028 the minimum age at which people can access their private pensions is expected to increase from 55 to 57, when the state pension age is increased to 67. So if you were born on or after 6 April 1973, you may have to wait at least another two years before you can tap your savings.

The minimum pension age is then expected to increase in line with the state pension age, always staying 10 years below state pension age. The state pension age is expected to increase to 68 between 2037 and 2039, which means the minimum pension age could then increase to 58. In the decades that follow the state pension age is expected to increase to 69 and then 70, although precise forecasts are impossible.

The increase in the minimum pension age from 55 to 57 in 2028 was announced in the Government's 2014 *Freedom and choice in pensions* consultation. So far the age increase has not been put into legislation and a future Government could leave the minimum age at 55, although this seems unlikely.

Proposals to Increase the Pension Age Sooner

It is possible the minimum pension age will be raised even faster. In March 2015 the Works and Pensions Committee stated that:

*"... the minimum age at which people can access their pension saving, except on ill health grounds, should rise to **five** years below the State Pension age."*

Presumably they were recommending raising the minimum age from 55 to 60 immediately.

And as recently as March 2020 there was fresh speculation in the media that Chancellor Rishi Sunak was under pressure to raise the minimum age to 57 as soon as possible. However, like so much speculation about pension changes in the media, this rumour turned out to be false.

Personally, I think the minimum pension age will be increased to 57 in 2028 but not before that. Forcing individuals to wait longer than expected to access their retirement savings would be extremely cruel and cause significant political damage.

However, the pension age debate does bring us neatly to one of the major drawbacks of pensions: almost every benefit can be taken away by politicians at the stroke of a pen.

They can change the age limits and tax reliefs, restrict how you invest your savings and make withdrawals and increase the tax paid on the money you take out or leave to your family.

Recent changes have definitely been for the better; future ones could be for the worse – politicians love to make gifts and then take them back!

Pension Freedom

When you're 55 (or probably 57 from 2028) you can start tapping your pension. You can take out as much money as you like, whenever you like.

You can withdraw the whole lot in one go or leave your entire pension pot untouched and give it to your family when you die (see Chapter 10).

Most people will probably do something in between these two extremes. For example, when you're 55 you could take your tax-free lump sum and leave the rest of your savings to grow tax free until you retire and then start withdrawing income gradually.

Saving tax will be a key consideration (see Chapter 11).

Under the new rules you can use one or more of the following products to access your pension:

- Flexi-access drawdown
- Uncrystallised funds pension lump sum (UFPLS)
- Lifetime annuity

Flexi-access drawdown lets you take your entire tax-free lump sum in one go and place your remaining savings into drawdown, where the money can be accessed as and when you like.

Taking an uncrystallised funds pension lump sum allows you to take your tax-free lump sum in stages instead of in one go. Like drawdown, you can make withdrawals as and when you like but one quarter of every withdrawal will be tax free with the remainder taxed as income.

Annuities have always been on the menu but are extremely unpopular these days because they pay a miniscule amount of income. They're also unpopular because the life insurance company generally confiscates your pension savings when you die or your spouse dies. Despite their drawbacks, annuities do nevertheless provide a guaranteed "risk-free" income for life, unlike drawdown and UFPLS.

The various income options are discussed further in Chapter 8.

Final Salary Pensions

The pension freedom reforms apply to "defined contribution" pensions only: personal pensions and SIPPs and many occupational pension schemes in the private sector.

They're not available to members of final salary pension schemes (also known as defined benefit schemes). Members of these schemes cannot withdraw as much money as they like, whenever they like.

However, if you belong to a final salary scheme it may be possible to transfer to a defined contribution scheme (e.g. a SIPP) and collect a large cash lump sum.

This is currently a "hot topic" for members of defined benefit pension schemes because transfer values of around 25 to 40 times the annual pension have been offered in recent times. So someone who expects to receive a pension of, say, £25,000 per year could have been offered a lump sum well in excess of £600,000.

Transferring to a personal pension may also allow you to access your pension savings earlier (for example, at age 55 instead of at age 60 or 65) and leave surplus funds to your children.

However, pension transfers are also highly controversial, which is why professional advice is necessary.

Many pension experts advise against transferring from a "gold-plated" final salary scheme, which offers a guaranteed income for life, to a "crummy" personal pension, where your retirement income will depend on how well your investments perform. Members of final salary schemes do not have to worry about the ups and downs of the stock market!

Members of unfunded public sector pension schemes (i.e. teachers, NHS employees and civil servants) are not able to transfer to a defined contribution scheme and access their pension as a lump sum. Unfunded pension schemes are ones that don't have any assets – they rely on taxpayers to keep up the pension payments.

Members of funded public sector schemes (such as the local government pension scheme) are able to transfer to a defined contribution scheme.

Tax on Pension Withdrawals

Although you can take one quarter of your pension savings as a tax-free lump sum, you have to pay income tax on everything else you withdraw, *including your original contributions*.

That's a bit like putting £100 in a bank account and paying £20 or maybe £40 tax when you withdraw the money a year later. Of course, this doesn't happen when you withdraw money from your bank account – at most you will pay tax on your interest.

So while pensions offer several tax concessions, there is a tax sting at the end.

Thus, the sixty-four-thousand dollar question is this:

Do the tax benefits – tax relief on contributions and tax-free investment growth – outweigh the penalty of taxed withdrawals?

In most cases the answer is "Yes". This is because most people will probably pay no more than 20% tax on the money they take out but will enjoy 40% tax relief when they put their money in, if they are higher-rate taxpayers.

Furthermore, some of the money you take out will be tax free, including your tax-free lump sum and any withdrawals that are covered by your income tax personal allowance.

This is why even basic-rate taxpayers will usually also end up better off with a pension. Although they only enjoy 20% tax relief when they put their money in, a significant chunk of the money they take out will be tax free.

But *exactly* how much better off are you likely to be with a pension? The benefits surely have to be significant to justify putting your money into a locked box until you're 55 or older.

One way to answer this question is to compare two investors: one putting money into a pension and the other putting money into a different tax shelter, an ISA, and see who ends up better off at the end of the day. We do this in Chapter 15.

Like pensions, money in ISAs grows tax free. However, unlike pensions, ISAs do not offer any upfront tax relief but all your withdrawals are tax free and your money is not tied up until age 55 or later – you can withdraw it whenever you like.

However, the problem with using ISAs as retirement saving vehicles is they give you tax relief when you may need it least. It's usually better to have 40% tax relief when you put your money in, as you do with pensions if you're a higher-rate taxpayer, rather than 20% tax relief when you take it out, as you would with ISAs (most individuals only pay 20% tax when they retire).

If you're under 40 you can now also invest in a Lifetime ISA. These arguably offer the best of both worlds: upfront tax relief (in the shape of a Government bonus) and tax-free withdrawals. We also compare Lifetime ISAs and pensions in Chapter 15.

Pension Advice

The Pensions Advice Allowance allows you to withdraw £500 tax free from your pension pot on three occasions (i.e. three separate tax years) to pay for pensions and retirement advice. The allowance is available at any age and to members of defined contribution pension schemes (not final salary pension schemes). Not all pension providers offer this facility, however.

Chapter 8

Flexi-Access Drawdown & UFPLS

If you want to make use of the new flexible regime for pension withdrawals you have two choices:

- Flexi-access drawdown
- Uncrystallised funds pension lump sum (UFPLS)

Some pension providers will only offer very limited options so you may have to shop around and, in some cases, it may even be necessary to transfer your pension to another provider.

Flexi-Access Drawdown

When you reach pension age (currently 55) you can move some or all of your pension savings into flexi-access drawdown.

One quarter (25%) can be taken as a tax-free cash lump sum and only flexi-access drawdown allows you to take your tax-free lump sum on its own without any additional taxable income (for example, if you want to withdraw some cash to pay down your mortgage before you stop working).

The remaining 75% continues to grow tax free in your drawdown fund until you withdraw it. You can withdraw as much income as you like whenever you like. All withdrawals will be fully taxed.

If at any point you decide you want a more secure income for the rest of your life, you can use some or all of your remaining drawdown funds to buy an annuity.

Phased Drawdown

If you don't want to take your entire tax-free lump sum in one go, you can use something called phased drawdown. For example, you may wish to withdraw a small tax-free lump sum to reduce your mortgage or for home improvements.

Phased drawdown may also appeal to those who are semi-retired. It allows you to make regular tax-free withdrawals to supplement your income before you are fully retired.

Then when you stop working completely (and your tax rate is hopefully lower) you can start withdrawing money from the taxable portion of your pension pot.

By not withdrawing your entire lump sum in one go it can continue to grow tax free inside your pension. As a result you may end up with more tax-free cash overall.

Example
Stacey is 58 and still working and has a pension pot worth £200,000. She wants to take just £10,000 out of her pension tax free. She transfers £40,000 into a flexi-access drawdown plan and takes the 25% tax-free lump sum of £10,000 and leaves the remaining £30,000 in the drawdown plan without taking any additional taxable income.

A couple of years later she transfers another £40,000 into the drawdown plan and takes another £10,000 of tax-free cash. She leaves the remaining £30,000 in the drawdown plan, along with the other £30,000 from two years ago.

She can keep doing this until she has transferred all of her pension pot into flexi-access drawdown.

Uncrystallised Funds Pension Lump Sum (UFPLS)

The recent pension reforms were clearly made in a hurry. How else can you explain calling something an "uncrystallised funds pension lump sum", with the unwieldy acronym UFPLS?

With UFPLS you can take your entire pension pot as a lump sum in one go, or take a series of smaller lump sums. Each lump sum will have a 25% tax-free element, with the rest taxed as income.

UFPLS may appeal to those who don't need all their tax-free cash immediately. Instead it can continue to grow tax free. Note, however, that a similar result can be achieved with flexi-access drawdown by using phased drawdown (if your pension provider offers it) and crystallising just a portion of your retirement savings.

Example

Zach has a £100,000 pension pot. He withdraws £20,000 using UFPLS, leaving £80,000 untouched. £5,000 of the UFPLS is tax-free cash, the remaining £15,000 is taxable. If we assume Zach has other income and is a basic-rate taxpayer he will pay 20% tax: £3,000. Zach can continue to use UFPLS to take lump sums as and when he needs. He can also move his remaining pension pot into flexi-access drawdown or, if he wants a secure income for the rest of his life with no investment risk, he can use his remaining funds to buy an annuity.

With UFPLS you have to take tax-free cash and taxable income at the same time – every withdrawal will consist of 25% tax-free cash and 75% taxable income.

Flexi-access drawdown is therefore more flexible because it lets you take tax-free cash without having to take any taxable income. This may be more appealing if you want to withdraw cash while you are still working and paying 40% tax. You can postpone withdrawing taxable income until you retire and start paying tax at 20% (most retirees are basic-rate taxpayers).

The Money Purchase Annual Allowance (MPAA)

When you start withdrawing money from your pension pot you can continue making pension contributions but you may be subject to the money purchase annual allowance (MPAA).

The money purchase annual allowance used to be £10,000 but was reduced to £4,000 on 6 April 2017.

This change will have a significant impact on some individuals. Being limited to an annual pension contribution of just £4,000 (compared with the normal £40,000 annual allowance) will make it very difficult for those who have accessed their pension savings (perhaps through financial hardship) to rebuild them.

If you are subject to the money purchase annual allowance you also cannot carry forward any unused allowance from previous tax years.

Note that £4,000 is the maximum *gross* pension contribution you could make. The maximum cash you could invest personally would be £3,200. The taxman would add £800 of basic-rate tax relief to produce a gross pension contribution of £4,000.

If you use flexi-access drawdown and take your 25% tax-free lump but do not withdraw any additional taxable income, you get to keep your £40,000 annual allowance, i.e. you can keep making pension contributions just like anyone else.

However, as soon as you take any income from your drawdown fund the money purchase annual allowance will apply.

With uncrystallised funds pension lump sums (UFPLS) the money purchase annual allowance applies once you start making any pension withdrawals. In other words, as soon as you start withdrawing money using UFPLS your pension contributions could be restricted to £4,000 per year.

Thus, flexi-access drawdown may be more suitable for those who want to keep making pension contributions. You can withdraw some or all of your tax-free cash and keep making pension contributions of up to £40,000 per year and use your unused annual allowance from the previous three tax years.

The money purchase annual allowance was introduced to reduce pension recycling – taking income out of a pension and using it to make fresh contributions with tax relief.

It is also designed to prevent those aged 55 and over replacing their regular taxed salaries with employer pension contributions, 25% of which could be withdrawn tax free immediately.

Note that additional rules prevent tax-free lump sums being recycled (see Chapter 9).

The MPAA only applies to money purchase pension contributions (e.g. those paid into personal pensions and SIPPs). It does not restrict contributions to defined benefit pension schemes (final salary schemes).

In other words, your annual allowance for funding a final salary scheme will generally still be £40,000, less any money purchase contributions within the £4,000 limit.

The money purchase annual allowance also isn't triggered if:

- You use your pension savings to buy a standard lifetime annuity

- You are using capped drawdown (the old type of drawdown that is no longer available to new retirees) and do not withdraw income above the maximum income limit

- You cash in a small pension pot. You can take up to three pension pots worth up to £10,000 each (an unlimited number from occupational pension schemes)

PAYE Issues

When you withdraw income from your pension, the pension provider will deduct tax before paying you.

If your pension provider does not hold a current P45 form for you (usually only issued when you stop working), tax will be deducted at the so-called emergency rate. In many cases this will mean that far too much tax is deducted and you will be due a refund.

For example, if you withdraw £10,000 from your pension at the start of the tax year you could be taxed as if your total income is £120,000 for the year.

The refund can be claimed at the end of the tax year or you can claim the tax back during the year (apparently within 30 days).

If you decide to make a single withdrawal that does not empty your pension pot, you can claim back the tax overpaid by completing a P55 form.

Those intending to make a series of irregular withdrawals are advised to talk to their pension providers. After applying emergency tax to the first payment, the pension provider might be able to report a zero payment for the months where no withdrawal is made and correct the tax deducted on subsequent withdrawals.

Another form P50Z is to be used if you empty your entire pension pot in a single withdrawal and have no other PAYE or pension income (other than your state pension). Form P53Z should be used if you have other employment income or pensions.

Chapter 9

The Pension Recycling Rules

When you start withdrawing income from a flexi-access drawdown plan or make any withdrawal using UFPLS, you will be subject to the money purchase annual allowance.

This may limit your future money purchase pension contributions to £4,000 per year and prohibit you from carrying forward any unused annual allowance from previous tax years.

If you use flexi-access drawdown and withdraw your tax-free lump sum only (with no additional income) you can continue making pension contributions of up to £40,000 per year (if you have sufficient earnings) and use any unused annual allowance from the previous three tax years.

However, if you use your tax-free lump sum to make new pension contributions, you have to be wary of HMRC's recycling rules. These are designed to prevent tax-free cash being reinvested in a pension and enjoying a second round of tax relief.

Example
Toby is 59, still working and a higher-rate taxpayer. Over the last 10 years he has been making pension contributions of £6,000 per year. Using flexi-access drawdown he withdraws £10,000 of tax-free cash in order to reinvest it in a pension. The taxman adds £2,500 of basic-rate tax relief, giving him a total gross pension contribution of £12,500. Furthermore, when he submits his tax return he receives higher-rate tax relief of £2,500.

Unfortunately for Toby his pension contribution may fall foul of HMRC's recycling rules which are designed to prevent you making larger than normal pension contributions because you have received a tax-free lump sum.

The recycling rules can even apply if you make bigger than normal pension contributions *before* you withdraw tax-free cash.

If the recycling rules apply, your tax-free lump sum will be treated as an unauthorised payment, resulting in a tax charge of up to 70%.

The recycling rules apply when ALL of the following conditions are met:

- You receive a pension commencement lump sum (tax-free lump sum)

- The tax-free cash, including any tax-free cash taken in the previous 12 months, exceeds £7,500

- Because you took tax-free cash your pension contributions are significantly larger than they otherwise would be

- The additional contributions are more than 30% of the tax-free cash

- The recycling was pre-planned

Point 2 means that small amounts of recycling effectively fall under the radar.

Example
Using phased drawdown Justine takes a tax-free lump sum of £7,000 and immediately invests all of it in a pension plan, producing a gross pension contribution of £8,750 after basic-rate tax relief is added. She hasn't received any other tax-free cash in the previous 12 months so the pension contribution does not fall foul of the recycling rules, even though the recycling was pre-planned.

Looking at point 3, for the recycling rules to apply there must be a significant increase in your pension contributions. This includes contributions made by you and your employer.

HMRC will look at your contribution history to determine if there has been a significant increase. If you haven't made any pension contributions for a while, your last contribution may be adjusted for inflation to produce a current value for comparison purposes.

As a rule of thumb, HMRC may argue that your pension contributions have increased significantly if they are 30% larger than they would have been without the tax-free cash.

HMRC doesn't just look for big pension contributions in the tax year you receive tax-free cash. They will also look at contributions made in the two tax years before you received the cash and in the two tax years after you took the cash.

Example
Harvey is 60 and for the last five years has been making pension contributions of £10,000 per year. He takes a £40,000 tax-free lump sum from his pension and uses some of it to pay for a new kitchen and the rest to make a £25,000 pension contribution in the next tax year. Because his pension contribution is more than 30% larger than those made in recent years he may fall foul of the pension recycling rules.

The amount of additional contributions is measured on a cumulative basis which means you may be caught out even if you only make relatively small additional pension contributions after receiving your tax-free cash.

Example
Joan has been making pension contributions of £10,000 per year for the last 10 years. She takes £20,000 of tax-free cash from her pension and uses some of it to increase her pension contributions as follows:

	Contribution	*Increase*	*% Increase*
Current year	*£12,500*	*£2,500*	*25%*
One year later	*£12,500*	*£2,500*	*25%*
Two years later	*£12,500*	*£2,500*	*25%*
Cumulative increase		*£7,500*	*75%*

Joan's pension contributions have not increased by more than 30% in any single year but the cumulative increase is 75%. This is more than 30% which means there has been a significant increase.

Because the additional pension contributions were pre-planned she may have to pay £14,000 tax on the £20,000 tax-free lump sum.

Turning to point 4, you'll only be caught by the recycling rules if your additional contributions are more than 30% of your tax-free lump sum. In Joan's case her additional contributions were £7,500 and are more than 30% of her tax-free lump sum (£20,000 x 30% = £6,000).

However, if her additional contributions were less than £2,000 per year (less than £6,000 in total) this would presumably not count as pension recycling.

Point 5 is the most vague. The recycling must be pre-planned which means you must have intended to take your tax-free lump sum to make significantly greater pension contributions.

If you decide to use your tax-free lump sum to significantly increase your pension contributions but make the contributions *before* receiving your tax-free lump sum this will also be treated as pre-planning (for example, if you use other savings or a loan to pay the contributions and then use your lump sum to replenish those savings or pay off the loan).

Where, on the other hand, you take a lump sum and only later decide to use it to make bigger contributions, there is no pre-planning.

When the Recycling Rules Do Not Apply

The key is that the recycling rules only apply when your pension contributions are significantly increased "because of" the tax-free lump sum.

There are other reasons why your pension contributions may increase significantly from year to year and they will not constitute recycling.

For example, let's say you increase your pension contributions from £10,000 to £15,000 in the year you take tax-free cash. Although your pension contributions have increased by more than 30% this may be because you've received a bonus or the profits of your business have increased or because you have more income taxed at 40% and want to maximise your higher-rate tax relief.

As long as you can demonstrate that, although your pension contributions have fluctuated, they are calculated on a consistent basis (e.g. as a percentage of your income) the recycling rules should not apply.

The recycling rules will also not apply if you make significantly larger pension contributions because you receive a cash windfall such as an inheritance.

Example
Sadie takes tax-free cash from her pension. A few months later her father dies leaving her a substantial inheritance. Because of the inheritance (and not because she received a pension lump sum), she decides to make larger than normal pension contributions. She invests the whole inheritance in her pension. These pension contributions will not constitute recycling because she did not pre-plan to use the pension lump sum to make significantly larger pension contributions.

In summary, it is probably possible to trickle some of your tax-free lump sum back into a pension, providing the additional annual contributions are very small and made over many tax years.

However, it's important to stress that this is high-risk tax planning because if you get it wrong the penalties are severe.

Anyone thinking of making larger than normal pension contributions a couple of years before or after taking tax-free cash should probably seek professional advice.

Chapter 10

Leaving Your Pension Pot to Your Family

Pensions have become a lot more attractive when it comes to leaving money to your family.

After you die your pension pot can be transferred tax free to any member of your family (or anyone else for that matter).

The new rules have applied since 6 April 2015.

Under the old rules, a 55% "death tax" was generally payable, leaving just 45% for your family.

The 55% tax could be avoided by using your pension savings to provide a "dependant's pension" for your spouse or children under 23. Of course, most people die when their children are over 23, so it usually wasn't possible to leave pension savings to children without paying the death tax.

The rules were more generous if you died before age 75 – your entire pension pot could be paid out tax free to your family... *but only if you hadn't started taking out any money.*

The New Rules

Death before Age 75

Your pension savings can be paid tax free to any beneficiary. It doesn't matter whether you've started withdrawing money or not.

Your beneficiaries can take the money as a tax-free lump sum or keep the money invested in a drawdown plan and make tax free withdrawals as and when they like – they don't have to wait until reaching the minimum pension age (currently 55).

The drawdown investments will continue to grow tax free until income is withdrawn.

Lump sum death benefits are only tax free if paid out within two years of the pension scheme administrator becoming aware of the member's death. Similarly, where uncrystallised pension savings are placed into flexi-access drawdown, withdrawals will only be tax-free if the drawdown designation is made within two years.

75 or Older

The 55% death tax has been abolished which means your beneficiaries can inherit all of your pension savings.

They will still have to pay income tax on any money they withdraw, just like you would, but they can also keep the money invested where it will continue to grow tax free for as long as they like, perhaps until they themselves retire.

There are no restrictions on the amount of income they can withdraw, i.e. the whole pension pot can be paid out in a single tax year, although this may not be very tax efficient.

Example
Helen dies aged 80, leaving pension savings of £100,000. Her son Kevin is her nominated beneficiary. He earns a salary of £60,000 per year. Helen's pension savings are placed into a drawdown plan for Kevin and he withdraws all the money as income during the current tax year.

Kevin will end up paying additional tax of £45,500 on the pension withdrawal. This is because his income for the year is now £160,000 which means he loses his income tax personal allowance and pays 45% tax on some of the pension withdrawal.

It may be more tax efficient for Kevin to leave the money growing tax free in the drawdown plan until he himself retires and then start making gradual withdrawals which will probably be taxed at 20%.

Inheritance Tax

It's important to point out that your pension savings are typically held in trust outside your estate and are thus free from inheritance tax in most cases.

This is because the administrator of the pension scheme normally has discretion over who gets the money, although they will typically be guided by your wishes, which can be stated by completing a simple expression of wishes form.

Because these forms are usually not legally binding (although rarely ignored), your pension savings will not form part of your estate for inheritance tax purposes.

Note, not all pension monies will escape inheritance tax. For example, an inheritance tax charge may arise if you make unusually large pension contributions because you are in ill health and then die within two years. (An individual may do this to try to take some of their assets out of the inheritance tax net.)

Note, if you make pension contributions while you are in normal health there will be no inheritance tax consequences.

Where contributions are made more than two years before death HMRC will assume that you were in normal health, unless there is evidence to the contrary.

An inheritance tax charge may also arise if you transfer from one pension scheme to another while in ill health and then die within two years of making the transfer.

Some people transfer from final salary schemes to personal pensions to increase the death benefits payable. There are also non-tax reasons for making such transfers.

In one recent tax case the Court of Appeal agreed with HMRC that a pension transfer by a person in ill health gave rise to an inheritance tax transfer of value. The main reason for the transfer was to prevent an ex-husband gaining access to the pension savings. However, the taxpayer's decision to not withdraw money from the pension enhanced the death benefits payable to her sons and gave rise to a transfer of value.

Nest & Inheritance Tax

Nest is the pension scheme set up by the Government to handle auto-enrolment. It has over eight million members.

Death benefits paid from Nest used to always form part of the member's estate for inheritance tax purposes. This was because members could only nominate a beneficiary, with no discretion. Nest members can still nominate a beneficiary and this means the retirement pot will be paid to the person nominated and will usually form part of the estate for inheritance tax purposes.

Nest members can now also make an expression of wish which means that their wish and current circumstances will be considered when Nest decides who the money goes to. As a result, the pension pot won't usually be subject to inheritance tax.

Tax Planning

With the 55% death tax abolished, combined with an exemption from inheritance tax in most cases, pensions are powerful vehicles for passing wealth tax free from one generation to another.

The assets in the plan will continue to grow tax free and the only tax payable by your beneficiaries will be income tax on withdrawals. They won't pay any income tax on their withdrawals if you die before age 75.

Your nominated beneficiaries (e.g. your children) can then pass on any unused funds to their own nominated beneficiaries (e.g. your grandchildren) and so on.

The grandchildren will pay tax on their withdrawals if your children die after reaching age 75. No tax will be payable if your children die before age 75.

Preserving Your Pension Pot

Because pension pots are potentially useful inheritance tax shelters, some advisers recommend that wealthy retirees who are worried about inheritance tax should consider using up their other assets before withdrawing income from their pensions.

For example, after you have withdrawn your tax-free lump sum you could place the rest of your pension savings in a drawdown plan and leave most of it growing tax free for your family. You could then use your other assets to fund your retirement, e.g. rental properties and ISAs.

Of course, most retirees cannot afford to leave all their pension savings intact. But most will have at least some pension savings left to pass on to family members.

So for almost everyone it is good news that the 55% death tax has been abolished. It put some people off making significant pension contributions and put some retirees under pressure to withdraw income from their pensions as quickly as possible, with potentially adverse income tax consequences.

Minimising Tax on Withdrawals

Parents who wish to pass on their pension pots to their children may need to teach them how to withdraw money tax efficiently. For a pension to be an effective inter-generational tax shelter it's important your beneficiaries' withdrawals are taxed at 20% or less.

This isn't a problem if you die before age 75 because your beneficiaries (e.g. your children) will be able to withdraw the money tax free. However, there are still things they can do to produce a better financial outcome.

For example, if your children aren't worried about their own inheritance tax it may be more tax efficient for them to withdraw all the money tax free rather than pass on the pension pot to your grandchildren, who will have to pay income tax on their own withdrawals (if your children die after reaching age 75).

Your beneficiaries could also withdraw money from your pension pot to fund pension contributions of their own. With higher-rate tax relief this could leave them significantly better off overall.

If you die after reaching age 75 the withdrawals made by your beneficiaries will be taxed. However, tax-free withdrawals can be made if your beneficiaries have no other income and the withdrawals are covered by their income tax personal allowances (currently £12,500). This may be the case if they are at university, starting a business or taking time off work to raise children.

Withdrawals taxed at just 20% can be made while your beneficiaries are basic-rate taxpayers as long as their pension withdrawals do not take them over the higher-rate threshold – currently £50,000 (£43,430 in Scotland).

Example
Andrew, age 74, dies with £200,000 left in his pension plan. His wife Diane, age 70, is his beneficiary. She decides to keep the money in a drawdown plan so that it can continue to grow tax free and remains outside her estate for inheritance tax purposes. She withdraws a tax-free income of around £15,000 per year until she dies aged 80. At this point there is £150,000 left in the drawdown fund.

Until recently Diane's daughter Brenda was her nominated beneficiary. Brenda is a successful GP and a higher-rate taxpayer. If she inherits the pension pot she will pay 40% tax on any withdrawals.

So a few years ago Brenda encouraged Diane to nominate her two grandchildren as beneficiaries. They are currently aged 18 and 20 and at university. Thanks to Brenda's forward thinking, the grandchildren can withdraw tax-free income each year to use up their income tax personal allowances and help them through university. Then when they start working they can continue withdrawing money and may only pay tax at 20% if they are basic-rate taxpayers. Alternatively they can keep the remaining savings invested tax free until they need it, possibly when they themselves retire if they are extremely prudent!

Nominating Beneficiaries

It's important to make sure your pension provider has an up to date expression of wishes form which is simple to complete and is used to nominate who should get your pension savings when you die. They can be used to nominate more than one person.

Chapter 11

How to Save Tax When You Tap Your Pension

When the pension withdrawal rules were relaxed there were fears that retirees would blow their pension savings on expensive holidays and Lamborghinis. A few reckless individuals will no doubt squander their savings but the vast majority will probably withdraw the money gradually and spend it wisely.

Nevertheless, there is still a danger that even careful retirees will spend their savings a bit too quickly and end up depleting their pension pots.

Those who want a guaranteed income for life, with no danger of running out of money, can always hand over their retirement savings to an annuity provider. For example, a 65 year old with a £200,000 pension pot can currently buy a guaranteed income for life of up to around £5,600 per year. This will increase in line with inflation and continue providing a pension for their widow.

It's not a lot but then again annuity rates are extremely low at present because interest rates are so low.

It may be possible to achieve a higher income by using a drawdown arrangement and investing in, for example, companies with a long track record of paying growing dividends, or other investments. However, your income will not be guaranteed and could fall, as could the value of your investments.

This is the dilemma retirees face in the wake of George Osborne's pension revolution. Freedom to spend your pension savings as you like does not necessarily buy you peace of mind.

You should probably only spend a tiny fraction of your pension savings each year if they are to last through your retirement. Some retirees may, however, wish to make bigger than normal withdrawals and this doesn't necessarily mean they're going to fritter the money away.

For example, you could make bigger than normal withdrawals to:

- Invest in tax-free ISAs
- Buy rental property
- Reduce your mortgage or other debts
- Start a business

One thing retirees no longer have to do is make bigger than normal pension withdrawals to avoid the 55% death tax (see Chapter 10). If anything, surplus money should remain invested in your pension pot for as long as possible so that it can be passed on to your family free from inheritance tax.

Tax will be an extremely important factor when it comes to deciding how much you withdraw from your pension and when. In this chapter we're going to take a closer look at some of the strategies pension savers may be able to follow to pay less income tax and capital gains tax.

For the first time, retirees have the freedom to control their tax bills to some extent, by making big pension withdrawals in some tax years and smaller withdrawals in others.

Saving Income Tax

Any money you withdraw from your pension, over and above your 25% tax-free lump sum, is subject to income tax. If you withdraw a lot in one go, you could end up paying tax at 40% or even 45%.

Most retirees should endeavour to pay no more than 20% tax on their pension withdrawals and one way to achieve this is by spreading withdrawals over many tax years.

During the current 2020/21 tax year you will pay no more than 20% tax if your taxable income from all sources is less than £50,000.

Most retirees do not earn more than £50,000 per year and should therefore refrain from making big pension withdrawals that push them into the 40% tax bracket.

In Scotland the higher-rate threshold is currently £43,430. At this income level the tax rate increases from 21% to 41%.

Example

It's the start of the 2020/21 tax year. Andrew is 60 and earns a salary of £60,000. He has been saving into a pension and ISA. His pension pot is worth £200,000 and his ISA savings are worth £100,000. His wife Elizabeth is the same age and has similar income and savings.

If for whatever reason Andrew decided to withdraw all of his pension savings in one go, one quarter (£50,000) would be tax free. The remaining £150,000 would be fully taxed. His total taxable income would be £210,000 (£60,000 salary plus £150,000 pension).

With this much income, all of his pension income would be taxed at either 40% or 45% and he would lose his income tax personal allowance.

Andrew's total income tax bill would rise from £11,500 (salary only) to £79,500. He would end up paying tax at an effective rate of 45.33% on his pension withdrawal.

Furthermore, the money he takes out would no longer grow tax free outside his pension plan.

Fortunately, Andrew has no need to tap his pension pot at this time and realizes he is better off leaving the money alone while he is working full time.

He doesn't even want to withdraw his tax-free lump sum because he has no use for it at present and wants it to continue growing tax free.

In fact, instead of taking money out, he intends to keep putting money into both his pension and ISA. He enjoys higher-rate tax relief on his pension contributions.

This is one of the reasons why pension savers need to be careful about tapping their savings too early. If you are using flexi-access drawdown and withdraw any income over and above your tax-free lump sum, your future pension contributions could be limited to just £4,000 per year (see Chapter 8).

A similar restriction applies if you withdraw any money as an uncrystallised funds pension lump sum (UFPLS).

Example continued

Three years later it's 2023/24 and Andrew is 63. He decides to resign from his job because he wants to work part time. His pension pot is now worth £270,000 and his ISA savings are worth £175,000. Before getting a part-time job he decides to take a year off to pursue various interests, including buying and renovating a rental property. Andrew and Elizabeth withdraw their 25% tax-free lump sums to purchase the property (£135,000 in total) and put the rest of their pension savings into drawdown plans.

Although the property will eventually produce _taxable_ income and capital gains (whereas the money was growing tax free inside their pensions), Andrew and Elizabeth believe they have found a genuine bargain which makes up for the loss of tax relief.

Because he has no other taxable income at present, Andrew withdraws an additional amount of around £12,500 tax free from his pension to avoid wasting his personal allowance. Based on current tax thresholds, he could also withdraw an extra amount of around £37,500 taxed at just 20%.

Because he has withdrawn _income_ from his pension, his future pension contributions will be limited to £4,000 per year. This does not cause Andrew any problems.

Example continued

A year later Andrew is 64 and gets a part-time job earning £15,000. He also earns £5,000 rent from his share of the property. If he doesn't need more income he can leave his pension pot to grow tax free. If he wants more income he can take at least another £30,000 taxed at just 20%.

Two years later Andrew is 66 and has reached state pension age and decides to stop working. His pension pot is now worth around £230,000 and his ISA savings have grown to over £200,000. Coupled with Elizabeth's savings and the income from the rental property, he feels financially secure enough to retire.

His state pension and rental income use up his income tax personal allowance so he will pay at least 20% tax on any income he withdraws from his pension in future. Keeping an eye on how his drawdown investments are performing, he varies the amount he withdraws each year but makes sure he never pays 40% income tax.

Reducing Capital Gains Tax

Because retirees can choose how much money they withdraw from their pension pots each year, they can halt or reduce withdrawals in years they sell assets like rental property and reduce their capital gains tax bills.

This is because you only pay 18% capital gains tax (as opposed to 28%) to the extent your basic-rate band is not used up by your income*. For example, in 2020/21 if you don't have any taxable income you can have £37,500 of capital gains taxed at 18%.

The potential tax saving is £7,500 per couple:

$$£37,500 \times 2 \times 10\% = £7,500$$

* Note these are the capital gains tax rates for residential property. The rates for other assets are now 10% and 20% respectively.

Example continued

Several years later Andrew and Elizabeth decide to sell their rental property because it has increased in value significantly and they don't want the hassle of managing tenants etc. They intend to use the proceeds to buy a holiday cottage.

After deducting various buying and selling costs and their annual CGT exemptions they expect to be left with taxable capital gains of £30,000 each. These amounts will be taxed at just 18%, providing they haven't withdrawn too much income from their pension pots.

In the tax year before the sale takes place they therefore decide to make larger than normal pension withdrawals, making sure they stay below the higher-rate threshold to avoid paying 40% tax.

In the tax year in which the property is sold they reduce their pension withdrawals so that all of their capital gains are taxed at 18%. They live off the extra income they withdrew during the previous tax year.

Once the sale has taken place, and they know how much of their basic-rate bands are left, they can withdraw some additional money from their pension pots taxed at just 20%.

Leaving Pension Wealth to Your Family

When you die your remaining pension savings can be left to your family (e.g. your spouse or children) who can keep the money growing tax free and make withdrawals as and when they like. The withdrawals will be subject to income tax if you die after reaching age 75.

When it comes to leaving pension savings to adult children, it is no longer necessary to deplete your pension pot to avoid the 55% death tax.

ISA savings can also be left to family members but only your spouse can effectively keep them in the ISA tax wrapper. For spouses this is a relatively new concession effective from 6 April 2015 (see Chapter 16).

Example continued
When Andrew dies at age 85 his remaining pension savings are left to Elizabeth. She also inherits his remaining ISA savings and is allowed to invest them in her own ISA.

Elizabeth now has two pension pots: her own and Andrew's. She wants to leave as much money as possible to her two children but she doesn't have to withdraw all her pension savings to avoid the 55% death tax.

Her remaining ISA savings can also be left to her children when she dies but the money will no longer be in a tax-free ISA and may be subject to inheritance tax.

One option would be to leave most of her pension savings intact and make tax-free withdrawals from her ISA to fund her living costs. This will reduce her estate for inheritance tax purposes.

If the children are likely to pay 40% income tax when they eventually inherit her pension savings, she could continue withdrawing income taxed at 20% in her hands and gift it to her children, although there may be inheritance tax consequences if she dies within seven years.

See the Taxcafe guide *How to Save Inheritance Tax* for more information about the various inheritance tax exemptions.

Withdrawing Lump Sums Gradually

Retirees who wish to make occasional large lump sum withdrawals should try to spread them over more than one tax year wherever possible.

Example
Barbara normally has income of £40,000, made up of rental income, state pension and withdrawals from her personal pension. In 2020/21 she wants to withdraw an additional £20,000 to pay for a log cabin garden office. If she withdraws all the money in 2020/21, £10,000 will be taxed at 40%. If she withdraws the money over two tax years she will pay tax at just 20%. Her total tax saving will be £2,000.

Big Contributions Close to Retirement

Because retirees can now make unlimited pension withdrawals, it may be worth making bigger than normal pension contributions when you are close to retirement.

Example
Alan and Betty are both 60 and each earn £65,000 per year. At present, they make gross pension contributions of around £5,000 per year each.

Betty's mother recently passed away, leaving her £80,000. Betty decides to give half the money to Alan so they can both ramp up their pension contributions before they stop working in five years' time. The reason Betty gives half the money to Alan and the couple spread their increased contributions over five tax years is so that higher-rate tax relief can be enjoyed on all of the additional contributions (see Chapter 4).

They're happy to make these increased pension contributions in the knowledge that the money will not be locked up in any way – they will be able to withdraw as much as they like, whenever they like.

They personally invest an additional £40,000 each over a five year period, making sure they always invest just enough to maximise their higher-rate tax relief (see Chapter 4). For example, in 2020/21 they will make an additional gross pension contribution of £10,000 each:

£65,000 income - £50,000 higher-rate threshold - £5,000 existing contribution

This means a cash pension contribution of £8,000 (£10,000 x 0.8).

Over the five year period the taxman will add £10,000 basic-rate tax relief to each pension pot, so they end up with additional pension savings of £50,000 each. They also enjoy additional tax refunds of £10,000 each (their higher-rate tax relief).

Ignoring any tax-free investment growth they enjoy on these additional pension contributions, when they retire they'll each be able to withdraw an additional tax-free lump sum of £12,500 (£50,000 x 25%).

The remaining money (£37,500 each) will be fully taxed when withdrawn. If we assume the withdrawals are taxed at just 20%, Alan and Betty will each be left with £30,000. Depending on how much other income the couple have, these taxed withdrawals may have to be made over several tax years to avoid paying tax at 40%.

In total Alan and Betty receive higher-rate tax relief of £20,000, tax-free lump sums totalling £25,000 and after-tax withdrawals totalling £60,000. So their £80,000 investment has grown to £105,000.

The reason Alan and Betty did so well is they spread their pension contributions over more than one tax year to maximize higher-rate tax relief and spread their withdrawals over more than one tax year to minimise their income tax bills.

It may also be worth making bigger pension contributions close to retirement even if you only enjoy basic-rate tax relief... but the benefits are far smaller.

Example
Emily is 60 and intends to retire next year. In recent years she has been investing just enough into her pension to maximise her higher-rate tax relief (see Chapter 4).

She has £24,000 sitting in a savings account and decides to invest all of it in her pension. The taxman adds £6,000 of basic-rate tax relief so she ends up with additional pension savings of £30,000. There is no higher-rate tax relief on this additional contribution.

Soon after retiring she decides to withdraw the whole £30,000. One quarter (£7,500) will be tax free. Emily pays 20% tax on the remaining £22,500, leaving her with £18,000. In total, Emily is left with £25,500, compared with her original investment of £24,000. So she enjoys a £1,500 windfall from this simple piece of tax planning.

What the above examples reveal is that, where possible, pension contributions should always be spread over several tax years if this means more higher-rate tax relief can be enjoyed.

Big pension contributions that only result in basic-rate tax relief may still be worthwhile in some cases but the benefits are modest.

You also have to watch out for HMRC's recycling rules. These are designed to stop you taking a tax-free lump sum and reinvesting it in your pension with a second round of tax relief (see Chapter 9).

The recycling rules can also be triggered if you make big pension contributions in the two tax years *before* you start withdrawing money.

HMRC says that very few lump sums will be affected and the recycling rules are only triggered if you always intended your tax-free lump sum to be an integral part of paying for your increased contributions (either directly or indirectly).

Retirees with Other Income

Retirees who are currently basic-rate taxpayers but expect to become higher-rate taxpayers in the near future, may consider making bigger pension withdrawals now to avoid paying tax at 40% in future.

Why would you expect to become a higher-rate taxpayer? Perhaps if you expect to receive a windfall (for example, an inheritance) or expect your income to grow faster than inflation.

Example
Ann is 75 and widowed and has income of £30,000 from her state pension and some rental properties. She also has a personal pension pot worth £200,000 from which she withdraws roughly £10,000 per year. Her total income is £40,000 so she only pays 20% tax.

Her mother Betty is 95 and lives in a nursing home. Ann expects to inherit all of Betty's assets when she dies, giving her additional taxable income of roughly £20,000 per year. With this extra income Ann will become a higher-rate taxpayer and will effectively pay 40% tax on the income she withdraws from her pension.

Before Betty dies Ann decides to withdraw an additional £10,000 per year from her pension and invest the money in an ISA where it will continue to grow tax free. She reasons that it is better to pay an additional £2,000 per year income tax now rather than £4,000 per year at some point in the future as a higher-rate taxpayer.

Although Ann may save income tax by making bigger pension withdrawals before becoming a higher-rate taxpayer, she may end up aggravating a more significant long-term tax problem she faces – inheritance tax.

When Ann eventually dies, 40% inheritance tax could be payable on a significant chunk of her assets: her rental properties, the money she inherited from her mother and the additional money she withdrew from her pension and invested in an ISA.

She'll be able to leave her remaining pension savings to her children or grandchildren free from inheritance tax, although they will pay income tax on any money they withdraw, possibly at 40% or more.

Ann could therefore consider gifting the additional money she withdraws from her pension to her children or grandchildren rather than invest it in an ISA.

Alternatively, she could consider halting all withdrawals from her pension after she inherits her mother's assets. This will allow her to avoid paying income tax at 40% and leave a bigger pension pot for her family to inherit.

Retirees with significant assets face a difficult juggling act deciding how much income to withdraw from their pensions to save both income tax and inheritance tax.

However, now that the 55% pension death tax has been scrapped they have considerably more flexibility and don't need to deplete their pension savings quickly.

Summary

- It is now possible to make unlimited pension withdrawals when you reach pension age (55 probably rising to 57 in 2028).

- Any money you withdraw over and above your tax-free lump sum will be subject to income tax.

- Most retirees pay no more than 20% tax and should avoid making withdrawals taxed at 40% or even 45%.

- This can be achieved by spreading withdrawals over many tax years, while keeping an eye on the higher-rate threshold (£50,000 in 2020/21, £43,430 in Scotland).

- Taxable lump sum withdrawals should be spread over more than one tax year where practical.

- In most cases it will not be tax efficient to withdraw income if you are still working and a higher-rate taxpayer.

- In some cases it may be worth postponing withdrawals so that capital gains are taxed at 18% instead of 28%.

- Money left inside your pension pot when you die is generally not subject to inheritance tax and is no longer subject to the 55% death tax.

- Your remaining pension savings can be left to anyone, e.g. your children or grandchildren. The money will continue to grow tax free but income tax will be paid on any withdrawals they make (unless you die before age 75).

Chapter 12

Pensions versus Buy-to-Let

Should you withdraw money from your pension to buy property?

This may be a good idea if you can earn a better *after-tax* return from property than from your *tax-free* pension investments (typically shares and bonds).

Investing in property has, however, become less attractive following two tax changes in recent years:

- 3% additional stamp duty land tax (4% in Scotland)
- A restriction to mortgage interest tax relief

Prior to April 2016 you wouldn't have paid any stamp duty land tax if you bought a rental property for £100,000... now you'll pay £3,000. You would have paid just £2,500 stamp duty if you bought a property for £250,000... now you'll pay £10,000!

When you add legal fees and mortgage arrangement fees, buying investment property is much more expensive than buying shares. With shares the stamp duty is just 0.5% and brokers' commission is often no more than a few pounds.

Thanks to the second tax change, borrowing to invest in property has become much more expensive for many landlords. Higher-rate tax relief for interest and other finance has now been taken away. Instead landlords are allowed a "tax reduction" equivalent to just 20% of their finance costs.

The tax relief restriction only affects *residential* property businesses and does not apply to properties held inside companies.

The restriction to tax relief on interest costs is even more painful than the stamp duty increase because those affected will feel its impact every year, not just when a new rental property is purchased.

See the Taxcafe guide *The Big Landlord Tax Increase* for more information about this tax change.

Example

Hannah is 55, a higher-rate taxpayer and has a pension pot worth £85,000. She decides to withdraw all the money to pay the deposits on two buy-to-let properties which she thinks will perform better than her pension investments over the next 10 years.

The first 25% she withdraws is tax free and the rest is taxed at 40%, leaving her with a grand total of £59,500. (Note, she will have to withdraw the money over more than one tax year to avoid going over the £100,000 threshold, which would result in an additional tax charge from the loss of her personal allowance. We will ignore this practical issue to keep the example simple.)

Using buy-to-let mortgages she acquires two properties for £100,000 each, with a £25,000 deposit and £75,000 mortgage on each property. The final £9,500 of her pension savings is used to cover her purchase costs (including stamp duty land tax of £6,000 and legal fees).

To be conservative and make the example even simpler we'll make the somewhat unrealistic assumption that she doesn't make any rental profit – all her rental income goes towards paying mortgage interest, income tax and other costs associated with the property.

We'll also assume Hannah's properties grow by roughly 7% per year. 10 years' later, when she's 65, they're worth £400,000 in total. She decides to sell one property to pay off both mortgages and use the second property for retirement income. On the £200,000 property she sells she faces a capital gains tax bill and other selling costs of roughly £20,000. After paying off both mortgages (£150,000 in total) she's left with £30,000 in the bank and a fully paid up property worth £200,000.

How would she have fared by keeping her pension investments instead? If we assume they also would have grown by roughly 7% per year, after 10 years she'd end up with around £170,000. She could withdraw 25% tax free and, assuming the rest was withdrawn gradually and taxed at just 20%, she would end up with £144,500 in total.

In summary, with property she ends up with £230,000, with a pension she ends up with £144,500.

Hannah does much better with property despite paying 40% tax on all the money she takes out of her pension to fund the purchases and despite the fact that she does not enjoy any rental profit and pays capital gains tax when she sells one of the properties.

Of course, the only reason the properties did better is because they were heavily geared up with borrowed money and grew handsomely in value. This is a very high-risk strategy and probably only suitable for experienced property investors who are many years away from retirement (i.e. closer to 55 than 65).

If the properties had fallen in value significantly, Hannah could have lost all of her capital.

What about using your pension savings to invest in property without a mortgage? Let's take a look at a simple example:

Example
Bill is 65 and retired and has a pension pot worth £150,000 (he has already taken his tax-free lump sum), as well as other taxable income of roughly £25,000 per year.

He currently withdraws the income generated by his pension investments but wants to keep the capital intact for his children. His pension savings are invested in funds earning income of £6,000 per year (£4,800 after paying 20% income tax). He wants to know if he could get more income by withdrawing all the money from his pension and buying a rental property outright without a mortgage.

If he withdraws all his pension pot in one go he'll pay 40% income tax on most of the money. He will also lose his personal allowance and some of the money will be taxed at 45%. So we'll assume he withdraws £50,000 per year over three tax years, paying 20% tax on around half his withdrawals and 40% tax on the rest, leaving him with £105,000.

He then buys a rental property for £100,000, using the final £5,000 to cover his stamp duty and legal fees. If the property is to earn more income than his pension investments (£6,000) it will need to have a rental yield significantly higher than 6%. That's because with property there are lots of additional costs (repairs, insurance, letting agent fees etc) and there are bound to be empty periods as well.

It is possible to find properties with higher rental yields (in some parts of the country they are higher, in others parts they are lower) but it's probably unlikely Bill will end up with *significantly* more income after deducting the various expenses he will incur.

The problem with using pension savings to buy an expensive asset like property outright is that it may be necessary to spread the withdrawals over many tax years to avoid paying income tax at 40% or more.

And what about Bill's children? When he dies they'll either inherit a pension pot worth £150,000 or a property worth £100,000, plus any capital growth on the investments. Whether they're better off with a pension pot or property will depend on Bill's inheritance tax status and the amount of income tax the children pay.

Let's say Bill's pension pot would be worth £225,000 when he dies after reaching age 75 and his property would be worth £150,000 (i.e. they would both grow by 50%).

If Bill's property is not subject to inheritance tax, his children will inherit the £150,000 asset outright, with no capital gains tax payable if they sell it immediately. Alternatively they will inherit his £225,000 pension pot with income tax payable on any withdrawals, leaving them with either £180,000 (if they pay 20% income tax) or £135,000 (if they pay 40% income tax).

If Bill's property is subject to 40% inheritance tax, his children will inherit £90,000. Alternatively they will inherit his pension pot and, as before, be left with either £180,000 (after paying 20% income tax) or £135,000 (after paying 40% income tax).

In this example the children are only better off with the property if there is no inheritance tax payable and they pay income tax at 40%. Of course, they wouldn't have to withdraw the pension savings immediately. The money could be left to grow tax free for as long as they like, perhaps until they themselves retire.

In summary, it is possible to deplete your pension savings to invest in property. However, this strategy is only likely to leave you better off if you're prepared to accept more risk (i.e. borrow money) or you expect property to deliver significantly higher returns than pension investments (typically shares and bonds).

Chapter 13

Drawdown versus Annuities

When you retire you may prefer to use your retirement savings to buy an annuity, rather than use flexi-access drawdown (see Chapter 8).

Annuities get a bad rap in the press but offer one important benefit: a guaranteed income for life. This may appeal to older retirees who don't want the hassle of managing investments and desire what is as close as it gets to a risk-free income.

Annuity rates are very low at present but may become more attractive if interest rates increase in the future. This is by no means certain and annuities may become even less attractive in future if only a small minority of retirees buy them (those who expect to live a long time).

Annuities are seen by many as a con. The idea is lots of retirees pool their money together and those that live longer than average are subsidized by those who live shorter than average. That's fair enough but what many people suspect is that annuity providers (typically insurance companies) skim off a big chunk of the money for themselves.

There are several other reasons why flexi-access drawdown may be more attractive than buying an annuity immediately:

Benefit #1 – Take the Tax-free Cash and Keep Working

When you reach age 55 you may want to get your hands on your 25% tax-free lump sum but keep working for another 10 years or even longer.

Any additional income you take from your pension pot while you are still working (e.g. annuity income) could be taxed at 40% or more if you also have income from a job or business.

Because there is no requirement to withdraw income from a flexi-access drawdown arrangement, you can postpone withdrawing income until you actually retire and your income tax rate falls.

While you are working your pension savings will continue to grow tax free.

Benefit #2 – Keep Your Favourite Investments

If you opt for an annuity you generally have to sell your pension investments and hand over your savings to an insurance company.

This is not an attractive proposition if you are confident your pension investments will perform well.

With a drawdown pension you can enjoy the best of both worlds: an income and tax-free investment growth on the money left inside your pension.

Benefit #3 – Wait for Better Annuity Rates

Many pension experts argue that you should ultimately use your pension savings to buy an annuity because the income is more secure than drawdown income (the income never falls no matter how long you live and no matter what happens to interest rates and the value of investments).

The problem is that annuity rates may be very low when you retire if interest rates are very low, as they are now. One solution is to start your retirement with a drawdown pension and make a phased exit by using part of your drawdown money to buy an annuity at regular intervals if interest rates rise and annuities become more attractive. Having said this, there are no guarantees that annuity rates will increase in the foreseeable future.

Benefit #4 – Reduce Your Income and Save Tax

If you can vary your income from year to year, as you can with drawdown, you can do a lot of constructive tax planning. This is very useful in years when your tax bill may spike because you receive big one-off receipts such as capital gains.

Let's say you sell a buy-to-let property and the capital gain is £50,000. If you reduce your drawdown income in the same tax year, so that your basic-rate band is not fully utilised, you will pay 18% tax instead of 28% tax on a big chunk of your capital gain.

The basic-rate band for 2020/21 is £37,500 so the maximum potential tax saving from paying 18% capital gains tax instead of 28% tax is currently:

$$£37,500 \times 10\% = £3,750$$

This tax saving could be enjoyed every time you sell a rental property and allows individuals with many properties to wind down their portfolios slowly when they retire.

Further capital gains tax savings can be achieved by spreading property sales across several tax years because this lets you make use of more than one annual CGT exemption. The potential additional tax saving in 2020/21 is £3,444 (£12,300 x 28%).

Annuities after Death

If you are receiving income from a bog-standard annuity, no money will be payable to your family (e.g. your children) after you die.

The income payments will continue if you have purchased a joint-life annuity (typically for your spouse) or an annuity which pays out for a guaranteed period.

The tax treatment has become more generous since 6 April 2015. If you die before age 75, payments made to your beneficiary will be tax free.

If you die when you are 75 or older, income paid to your beneficiary will be taxed at their marginal rate.

Part 3

Pensions vs ISAs

Chapter 14

Introduction

Which is better: an ISA or a pension?

This is an important question. ISAs and pensions are the two most popular savings vehicles for individuals.

When it comes to saving tax there are no ifs, buts or maybes: pensions are a **much** more powerful tax shelter for most higher-rate taxpayers.

With ISAs there is no up-front tax relief on the money you put in but withdrawals are tax free. With pensions there is up-front tax relief but most withdrawals are taxed.

At first glance the two tax reliefs appear quite different but, as it happens, tax-free withdrawals (ISAs) and up-front tax relief (pensions) produce exactly the same result, even though the tax savings are enjoyed at different points in time.

However, there are two reasons why pensions are a much better tax shelter, especially for higher-rate taxpayers:

- **Tax-free lump sum**. Not all of your pension withdrawals are taxed. You can take one quarter as a tax-free lump sum.

- **Retirees pay less tax**. If your tax rate falls from 40% to 20% when you retire – as it will for most higher-rate taxpayers – a pension could save you a lot more tax than an ISA. This is because you will enjoy 40% tax relief on the money you put in but will pay no more than 20% tax on the money you take out.

Thanks to these two factors it is quite possible that a pension will generate 41.67% more after-tax income than an ISA, as we shall see in Chapter 15.

Other Tax Differences

Apart from these major tax differences, pensions and ISAs are treated differently in other respects which may be important in some circumstances.

Interest on Cash Balances

While it has always been possible to hold cash in a stocks and shares ISA, any interest was in effect paid net of basic-rate tax. Interest earned in a pension has always been tax free.

Since July 2014 this has changed. Interest on cash held in a stocks and shares ISA is now completely tax-free.

Tax When You Emigrate

If you become non-UK resident your income and capital gains sheltered inside an ISA will continue to be tax free. Tax free in the UK, that is. The amounts may be taxed in your new country of residence. For example, the Isle of Man Government specifically states in its tax return booklet that an ISA's tax-free status "does not apply in the Isle of Man and you should declare any income from these products".

The tax-exempt status of pensions, however, is recognized in most countries, although they are arguably less portable assets (you can withdraw all your ISA savings easily if you emigrate).

Withholding Taxes on Dividends

These days it is easy for stock market investors to buy shares in overseas companies, the most popular being US companies. You have to be careful about doing this because the dividends are often subject to a withholding tax.

In the US, the dividend withholding tax rate is 30%. However, in terms of the double tax agreement between the US and UK, the amount of withholding tax can be reduced by completing an IRS form W-8BEN. Most online stockbrokers will handle these forms on your behalf so the process is relatively simple.

However, there is an important difference between US shares held inside a pension and an ISA. The double tax agreement provides a specific exemption for pension schemes, which means US dividends can be received tax free by UK pension savers.

The double tax agreement does not, however, recognize ISAs. ISA investors are subject to the same reduced withholding tax rate as everyone else: 15%.

ISAs – Protection from Greedy Politicians

Although pensions are arguably a better tax shelter, one tax benefit unique to ISAs is protection from future increases in income tax rates.

Money withdrawn from ISAs is tax free, whether those withdrawals take place next year or in 30 years' time. In contrast, if a future UK Government decides to increase income tax rates or reduce the threshold where 40% tax kicks in, it is quite possible you will pay more than 20% tax on your pension income.

In Scotland income tax rates have already been increased for some taxpayers – those who currently earn more than £27,243 pay more income tax than those who live in the rest of the UK. The Welsh Assembly has had the power to set its own tax rates since 6th April 2019 but has promised to not increase income tax during the current Assembly term – i.e. until May 2021.

It's impossible to predict what will happen to income tax rates in the years ahead. However, there's no denying that Britain has had its fair share of barmy taxes. In 1974 the top income tax rate on earnings was increased to 83% and the top rate on investment income was 98%.

Do you trust politicians to not increase your income tax at any time between now and the date you die? If not, then it may be a good idea to put some of your retirement savings into ISAs.

ISAs are not, however, completely immune from politicians. There have been rumours in the press in recent times about a lifetime cap being placed on ISA savings to limit the number of 'ISA millionaires'. Nothing has been announced to date.

Help-to-Buy ISA

In the 2015 Budget George Osborne introduced the Help to Buy ISA – a form of cash ISA where the Government adds £50 for every £200 saved towards a deposit for a first property. The maximum Government bonus is £3,000 for those who have saved £12,000.

It is no longer possible to open one of these accounts (the last date was 30 November 2019). However, those who have an existing account can continue contributing up to £200 per month until 30 November 2029.

Savers can withdraw funds from their account if they need them for another purpose but the bonus will only be made available to buy a home.

Lifetime ISA

Those aged 18 to 39 can open a Lifetime ISA which can be used to save for a first home or for retirement.

Any money you put in (up to £4,000 per year) receives a 25% Government bonus. So if you put in £4,000, the Government will add £1,000.

It's possible to continue making contributions up to age 50. This means you will be able to invest up to £128,000 between age 18 and 50 with a Government bonus of up to £32,000.

The bonus is paid monthly.

Contributions to a Lifetime ISA fall within the overall £20,000 ISA subscription limit. In other words, if you invest £4,000 in your Lifetime ISA you will be able to invest another £16,000 in a cash ISA or a stocks and shares ISA.

Lifetime ISAs are available from banks, building societies and investment managers and qualifying investments are the same as for cash ISAs and stocks and shares ISAs.

You can open more than one Lifetime ISA during your lifetime (as long you're under 40) but can only pay into one during each tax year.

Lifetime ISAs – Early Withdrawals

Unlike a pension, your savings are not locked up inside a Lifetime ISA. However, if you withdraw money before reaching age 60, for any reason other than to buy your first home, there will normally be a 25% early withdrawal charge.

This will claw back all of the Government bonus, plus an additional 6.25% of the amount you invested.

For example, if you invest £1,000, the Government will add £250, giving you total savings of £1,250. If you then decide to withdraw the money, the 25% penalty will normally be £312.50, leaving you with £937.50.

Thus you will lose the Government bonus plus an extra £62.50 (6.25%) out of the amount you originally invested.

This charge effectively also applies to any growth in the value of your savings.

Where an individual is diagnosed with terminal ill health, they will be able to withdraw all their Lifetime ISA savings tax free (including the bonus), regardless of age.

Note, the early withdrawal charge has been reduced temporarily from 25% to 20% for withdrawals taking place between 6 March and 5 April 2021.

This is to help individuals experiencing financial difficulty during the coronavirus crisis and means you will lose the Government bonus but will not face any additional penalty for now.

Lifetime ISAs – Buying Your First Home

If you are a first-time homebuyer, funds can be withdrawn 12 months after opening the account. The property must cost no more than £450,000, be located in the UK and your only residence.

The money cannot be used to invest in buy-to-let property.

The account holder will inform their ISA manager that a property is to be purchased and the funds will be paid direct to the solicitor.

If you already have a Help to Buy ISA you will only be able to use the Government bonus from one of the accounts to buy your first home.

If you have a Help to Buy ISA and a Lifetime ISA you could, for example:

- Use the Help to Buy ISA with the Government bonus to buy your first home and keep your Lifetime ISA to save for retirement

- Use the Lifetime ISA with the Government bonus to buy your first home and withdraw the money in your Help to Buy ISA (without the government bonus) to also fund the purchase

Lifetime ISAs – Saving for Retirement

If you use your Lifetime ISA to save for retirement, funds can be withdrawn from age 60.

As we shall see in Chapter 15, a Lifetime ISA could be an attractive alternative to saving in a pension if you are a basic-rate taxpayer. Like pensions they will attract a top up from the Government but, unlike pensions, ALL the money you take out will be tax free.

However, in most cases it would probably be unwise to stop making contributions to a workplace pension scheme because that would also mean giving up your employer's contribution (which is effectively 'free' money).

The Lifetime ISA will have the same inheritance tax treatment as other ISAs: when you die the funds will form part of your estate for inheritance tax purposes.

However, your spouse will be able to transfer all your ISA savings into their own ISA so that the money continues to grow tax free.

ISAs – Non-tax Benefits

- **Flexibility.** ISAs are extremely flexible investments that allow you to access your savings *at any time*. Since 6 April 2016 you can withdraw and replace cash from your ISA without it counting towards your annual ISA subscription limit, as long as the repayment is made in the same tax year as the withdrawal. At present pension savers can only access their money when they reach age 55 (probably rising to age 57 in 2028 and 58 at some point in the future). It's a fat lot of good having £100,000 sitting in your pension pot if you desperately need emergency cash.

- **No age limit**. In practice you cannot keep contributing to a pension indefinitely. Once you reach age 75 you will not receive tax relief on your contributions. There is no upper age limit for ISA investments and you can withdraw money and make new contributions continually.

- **No earnings required.** If you want to contribute more than £3,600 per year to a pension you need 'earnings'. There is no such restriction on ISA investments, although the maximum annual investment is currently capped at £20,000.

Pensions – Non-tax Benefits

- **Investment limits.** The maximum annual investment is £40,000 and the carry-forward rules allow a contribution of up to £160,000. However, as we saw in Chapter 4, the maximum contribution that you can make with full higher-rate tax relief is probably a lot lower than these limits.

- **Investment choice**. Pensions offer a wider choice of investments than ISAs. For example, ISAs cannot be used to invest directly in commercial property whereas pensions can.

- **Protection from creditors**. In the event of bankruptcy, pension savings held inside an HMRC approved pension are generally protected from creditors (most occupational and personal pensions are HMRC approved). Money withdrawn from a pension can potentially be claimed for a period of time.

Chapter 15

Case Study: ISA vs Pension

In this chapter we'll follow two investors building up a retirement nest egg over 10 years and see who ends up better off:

- Peter – Pension investor
- Ian   – ISA investor

Both are higher-rate taxpayers and invest £6,000 per year. Peter makes an initial contribution of £8,000 to which the taxman adds a further £2,000 in basic-rate tax relief.

He then claims back £2,000 when completing his tax return. All in all Peter has £10,000 of pension savings that have only cost him £6,000.

Ian also invests £6,000 per year out of his own pocket in an ISA. He doesn't get any tax relief on his contributions so his total investment is just £6,000. Note Ian invests in a traditional ISA. We'll compare pensions and Lifetime ISAs shortly.

Both Peter and Ian enjoy investment returns of 7% per year. These returns are completely tax free for both the ISA investor and the pension investor.

We track how both investors perform from year to year in Table 3. At the end of year 1 they have £10,700 and £6,420 respectively, which is simply their initial investments of £10,000 and £6,000 plus 7% tax-free investment growth.

After five years, Peter has £24,613 more than Ian and after 10 years he has £59,134 more than Ian. Even though they're both earning an identical tax-free return of 7% and investing the same amount of money out of their own pockets, Peter is much better off because his annual investment is boosted by income tax relief on his contributions.

In fact, Ian always has just 60% as much money as Peter. Peter's extra 40% is thanks to the income tax relief he receives on his pension contributions.

Table 3
Pension Savings vs ISA Savings

End Year	Pension £	ISA £
1	10,700	6,420
2	22,149	13,289
3	34,399	20,640
4	47,507	28,504
5	61,533	36,920
6	76,540	45,924
7	92,598	55,559
8	109,780	65,868
9	128,164	76,899
10	147,836	88,702

After-tax Comparison

Although Ian's retirement savings are much smaller than Peter's, that's not the whole story. Firstly, Ian enjoyed much more flexibility along the way and could have taken money out of his ISA at any time. Peter can only withdraw money from his pension when he's 55 or older.

Secondly, Ian can withdraw all his ISA savings *tax free*. Peter will have to pay income tax on any money he withdraws over and above his 25% tax-free lump sum.

If he withdraws all his pension savings in one go he'll end up paying tax at 40% on most of the money. However, because these are *retirement savings* we will assume that Peter only withdraws a little bit of money each year to avoid depleting his capital too quickly and therefore pays income tax at 20%.

But before we do this let's pretend Peter has to pay 40% tax on all his pension withdrawals and the pension rules do not allow for tax-free lump sums. How would ISAs and pensions compare then?

40% Tax, No Tax-Free Lump Sum

After paying 40% tax on all of his withdrawals Peter the pension saver would be left with £88,702:

$$£147,836 \text{ less } 40\% \text{ tax} = £88,702$$

Ian the ISA investor would also be left with £88,702:

$$£88,702 \text{ less } 0\% \text{ tax} = £88,702$$

Their after-tax positions would be *identical*. If you are a higher-rate taxpayer before and after you retire, an ISA and pension will provide identical tax savings – if you ignore the tax-free lump sum.

40% Tax, Tax-Free Lump Sum

Of course, in practice Peter can take a 25% tax-free lump sum of £36,959 (£147,836 x 25%). He'll only pay tax on the remaining £110,877.

If we assume he still pays 40% tax on the rest of his pension withdrawals his position after tax is as follows:

Tax-free lump sum:	£36,959
After-tax income (£110,877 less 40% tax):	£66,526

Peter is left with a total of £103,485 compared with Ian the ISA investor's £88,702.

This means Peter has 16.67% more money.

So even if you're a higher-rate taxpayer when you retire you will still receive more after-tax income from a pension than an ISA, thanks to the tax-free lump sum.

Although most retirees are basic-rate taxpayers, you could end up paying tax at 40% on some or all of your pension withdrawals if you have a significant amount of income from other sources (e.g. rental property). You could also end up paying tax at 40% on some of your withdrawals if you have built up a large pension pot and therefore have a large pension income.

20% Tax, Tax-Free Lump Sum

Finally, we'll assume that Peter, like most other retirees, is a basic-rate taxpayer when he retires. Peter's after-tax position is now as follows:

Tax-free lump sum: £36,959
After-tax income (£110,877 less 20% tax):   £88,702

Peter is left with a total of £125,661 compared with Ian the ISA investor's £88,702.

Peter the pension saver ends up with 41.67% more money than Ian the ISA investor.

This example shows that, if you are a higher-rate taxpayer while you are saving for retirement and a basic-rate taxpayer when you retire, you will end up significantly better off using a pension rather than an ISA to save for retirement.

Tax-Free Pension Withdrawals

In the above example Peter pays 20% income tax on all of his pension income. The implicit assumption is that his income tax personal allowance is used up by other taxable income, perhaps his state pension and income from rental properties or a part-time job or part-time business.

I taxed all of his private pension income at 20% because I did not want to overstate the benefits of pension saving. In reality, some of the income you receive from a private pension plan may be tax free thanks to your income tax personal allowance.

The income tax personal allowance for the current 2020/21 tax year is £12,500.

There used to be additional age-related personal allowances for older taxpayers but these have now been almost completely phased out.

Nevertheless, the sharp increase in the standard income tax personal allowance in recent years means that most retirees will continue to receive a significant proportion of their income tax free.

Once you reach state pension age your state pension could use up a big chunk of your personal allowance. However, you can start withdrawing income from your other pensions roughly 10 years earlier. If during this period your taxable income from other sources (e.g. rental property) does not use up all of your personal allowance, some of your pension income will be tax free.

If some of your pension income will be tax-free, this makes pensions even more attractive than ISAs for retirement saving.

Lifetime ISA vs Pension

Those aged 18 to 39 can now open a Lifetime ISA which can be used to save for a first home or for retirement.

It's possible to invest up to £4,000 per year with a £1,000 Government bonus and continue contributing up to age 50.

The Lifetime ISA is an attractive alternative to saving in a pension if you are a basic-rate taxpayer. Like pensions they attract a top up from the Government but, unlike pensions, ALL the money you take out will be tax free.

For example, if you are a basic-rate taxpayer and invest £1,000 in either a pension or a Lifetime ISA you will receive a £250 top up from the taxman, leaving you with £1,250 in either account.

When you retire, however, withdrawals from the Lifetime ISA will be tax free, whereas only 25% of the money withdrawn from the pension will be tax free. The rest will typically be taxed at 20% (although some of your pension income could also be tax free thanks to your personal allowance).

If we ignore investment growth to keep the example simple (it doesn't affect the outcome), with a Lifetime ISA you will end up with £1,250, with a pension you could end up with just £1,063 after tax.

Thus, if you're a basic-rate taxpayer, your retirement income could be 17.6% higher with a Lifetime ISA!

Lifetime ISA vs Pension – Higher-rate Taxpayers

Higher-rate taxpayers will generally get more bang for their buck with a pension.

For example, if you invest £1,000 in a Lifetime ISA you will receive a £250 top up from the Government leaving you with £1,250.

However, because higher-rate taxpayers also receive a tax refund when they contribute to a pension (higher-rate tax relief) they can make bigger initial contributions. For example, if you invest £1,333 in a pension (£1,000/0.75) you'll receive a £333 top up from the Government, leaving you with £1,666 in your pension.

You will also receive higher-rate relief of £333 (£1,666 x 20%) so, as with a Lifetime ISA, the investment will only cost you £1,000 personally (£1,333 personal investment - £333 higher-rate relief).

Ignoring investment growth, when you retire your £1,666 pension pot will become £1,416 (after taking 25% tax free and the rest taxed at 20%), compared with the £1,250 you would receive from a Lifetime ISA.

Thus, your retirement income could be 13% higher with a pension.

But if you are still a higher-rate taxpayer when you retire (for example if you have a lot of income from other sources, e.g. rental property) you will end up with only £1,166 from a pension, compared with £1,250 from a Lifetime ISA. Thus your retirement income could be 7% higher with a Lifetime ISA.

There are other important differences between Lifetime ISAs and pensions. With pensions your money is locked up until you're 55 (probably rising to 57 in 2028). With Lifetime ISAs you'll lose the Government top up and normally pay a penalty if you withdraw anything before age 60, unless the money is used to buy your first home. The rest of your savings can be withdrawn at any time.

If the pension is a company scheme, the additional contribution from your employer will make investing in such a scheme more attractive than a Lifetime ISA in most circumstances. In other words, you should probably not opt out of your employer's pension scheme to invest in a Lifetime ISA.

Make Mine a Double!

It *may* be possible to invest in a Lifetime ISA and then, when you're 60, take the money out and stick it into a pension, thereby enjoying two rounds of tax relief.

For example, if you invest £1,000 in a Lifetime ISA you will receive a 25% Government bonus, leaving you with £1,250. Ignoring investment growth, when you're 60 you will be able to withdraw the £1,250 tax free and may be able to invest it in a pension.

Because higher-rate taxpayers also receive a tax refund when they contribute to a pension (higher-rate tax relief), they can make bigger initial contributions. So instead of investing just your Lifetime ISA savings of £1,250 in your pension, you may be able to invest £1,667 (£1,250/0.75).

You'll receive £417 of basic-rate tax relief from the taxman, leaving you with £2,084 in your pension. You will also receive higher-rate relief of £417 (£2,084 x 20%), so the investment will only cost you £1,250 personally (the amount withdrawn from the Lifetime ISA).

Ignoring investment growth, when you eventually retire your £2,084 pension pot will become £1,771 (after taking 25% tax free and the rest taxed at 20%), compared with the £1,250 you would receive from your Lifetime ISA alone.

Thus, your retirement income could be 42% higher than someone who invests in a Lifetime ISA only.

And your retirement income will be 77% higher than someone who invests in a traditional ISA only (ignoring investment growth they would end up with just £1,000).

It's impossible to say whether anyone will be able to benefit from this potential "tax loophole".

Because only those who are under 40 can open a Lifetime ISA and because withdrawals will only be possible from age 60, it will be many years before anyone can perform this tax relief double! Tax and pension rules will no doubt change a lot between now and then.

Chapter 16

ISAs vs Pensions: Death Tax Planning

Your Spouse

There is no inheritance tax on assets, including ISAs, left to your spouse.

Thanks to a change that applies from 6 April 2015, your spouse can now inherit your ISA savings and invest them in their own ISA, so any future income and capital gains will continue to be tax free.

This was not possible before – your spouse could inherit your ISA savings but they were taken out of the ISA wrapper.

What happens now is your spouse will receive a special expanded ISA allowance when you die which will allow them to put all your ISA savings into their own ISA.

This tax concession is available to married couples and civil partners but not common-law spouses (i.e. unmarried couples).

How do ISAs compare with pensions?

Your spouse or common-law spouse can inherit your pension pot and withdraw money from it as and when they like. The investments inside the pension will continue to grow tax free.

If you die before age 75 your spouse or common-law spouse can withdraw all the money tax free. If you die after reaching age 75 they will pay income tax on any money they take out.

If your spouse or common-law spouse already has significant pension savings or other taxable income of their own and inherits a second pension pot from you, it is possible that any additional withdrawals they make from the second pension pot will take them over the higher-rate threshold and be taxed at 40%.

For this reason it may be preferable, in some cases, for married couples to run down their pension savings rather than their ISA savings, as long as no more than 20% tax is paid on the pension withdrawals.

The surviving spouse can then inherit a larger quantity of ISA savings and make tax-free withdrawals from them.

Unmarried couples who inherit ISA savings cannot keep them inside the tax wrapper. This means they may pay tax on any *future* income and capital gains. However, the original capital they inherit is tax free and can be spent without any tax consequences. Furthermore, your common-law spouse can gradually reinvest the money in their own ISA.

Passing on ISA savings may not be the most tax efficient route when it comes to leaving money to your children.

Your Children

When you die your ISAs will form part of your estate for inheritance tax purposes (although certain AIM shares are exempt after two years).

Inheritance tax at 40% is payable on assets that exceed the threshold – currently £325,000 but up to £650,000 for married couples. A new additional nil rate band, currently £175,000, is also available on the family home (up to £350,000 for married couples).

If your ISA savings are not subject to inheritance tax your children will effectively inherit a tax-free lump sum, although the money will be inherited outside the ISA tax wrapper.

If your children inherit your pension pot there is usually no inheritance tax payable. They can then withdraw money from it as and when they like. The investments inside the pension will continue to grow tax free.

If you die before age 75 your children can withdraw all the money tax free. If you die after reaching age 75 they will pay income tax on any money they take out.

If your children are working when they inherit your pension savings, there's a good chance they will end up paying 40% income tax on any money they take out, unless they leave the money untouched until they themselves retire (and pay tax at 20% possibly).

In summary, if your estate will not be subject to inheritance tax your children may be better off inheriting your ISAs rather than your pension.

If your estate is subject to inheritance tax they may be better off, pound for pound, inheriting your pension savings – but only if they will pay less than 40% tax when they take the money out.

Are ISAs Still a Good Investment?

In Chapter 15 it was shown that pensions are usually a much better tax shelter than ISAs (although the new Lifetime ISA will be better for some taxpayers). However, there are 17 million ISA savers in Britain and I'm one of them!

What attracts so many people to ISAs is their flexibility. You can withdraw money at any time. Pension investors have to wait until they reach the minimum retirement age of 55 or older.

As with everything in life, a compromise is usually the best solution. There's no harm in using both.

And as we will see in the next two chapters, an ISA may be a great place to park money **before** you invest it in a pension.

Part 4

Postponing & Accelerating Pension Saving

Chapter 17

Basic-Rate Taxpayers: Should They Make Pension Contributions?

Financial advisors usually advise people to start making pension contributions as early as possible. They often point to the 'magic' of compound interest. Compound interest – earning interest on interest – seems to possess magical powers, making millionaires out of just about anyone who starts early enough.

However, it's important to not confuse saving in a pension with saving *generally*. It's never too early to start saving... but it may be too early to start saving in a pension.

In previous chapters I have shown that higher-rate taxpayers enjoy twice as much tax relief on their pension contributions as basic-rate taxpayers. A higher-rate taxpayer is someone who has taxable income of more than £50,000 in 2020/21 (£43,430 in Scotland).

So the question is: should you delay making pension contributions if you are currently a basic-rate taxpayer but expect to become a higher-rate taxpayer in the future?

More specifically, should you invest your savings somewhere else, for example in a tax-free ISA, and transfer the money into a pension when you will enjoy much more income tax relief?

This is the question we will answer in this chapter.

Are You a Temporary Basic-Rate Taxpayer?

There are lots of reasons why an individual may be a basic-rate taxpayer in one tax year but a higher-rate taxpayer in another tax year.

The most obvious reason is career progression: a graduate earns a lot less income than someone with the same qualifications and

20 years' work experience. You may start your working life as a basic-rate taxpayer and become a higher-rate taxpayer a number of years later.

Many self-employed business owners who are normally higher-rate taxpayers may be basic-rate taxpayers from time to time, either because their incomes fall during tough economic conditions or because they have abnormally high tax-deductible expenditure during any given tax year, for example if they make significant investments in equipment.

Many company directors are also basic-rate taxpayers in some years but higher-rate taxpayers in other years, for example if they pay themselves a small dividend during one tax year and a big dividend during another tax year.

Wealth Warning

There is one group of individuals who should always consider making pension contributions, even if they are only temporary basic-rate taxpayers: company employees who belong to workplace pension schemes. For them tax relief is only one of the benefits of making pension contributions. The employer will often match, or more than match, the contribution made by the employee – effectively handing over free cash which no thrifty person would turn down (more on this in Chapter 22).

Case Study – Postponing Pension Contributions

Penny and Isabella are both basic-rate taxpayers but expect to be higher-rate taxpayers in three years' time. Both want to save £3,000 per year but they have different strategies. Penny decides to put her savings in a personal pension straight away because her father has advised her to start saving for retirement as soon as possible. Isabella also wants to save for her retirement but she also wants to maximise her tax relief. She decides to invest in an ISA until she is a higher-rate taxpayer and then transfer the money into a pension.

Who ends up better off?

Table 4
Pension vs ISA
Temporary Basic-Rate Taxpayers

End Year	Pension £	ISA £
1	4,013	3,210
2	8,306	6,645
3	12,900	10,320

We'll assume they both enjoy investment returns of 7% per year (tax-free inside both an ISA and pension). Penny's £3,000 annual investment is topped up with £750 of free cash from the taxman so her gross pension contribution is £3,750. After a year this will have grown to £4,013. After three years she will have £12,900.

Isabella's £3,000 ISA investment will be worth £3,210 after one year. After three years she will have £10,320. The results are summarised in Table 4. For every £1 Penny has in her pension, Isabella has just 80p – the difference is down to the 20% basic-rate tax relief Penny enjoys on her pension contributions.

Becoming Higher-rate Taxpayers

It's the start of the fourth tax year and Isabella knows she will be a higher-rate taxpayer this year. So she decides to take her £10,320 ISA savings and stick them into her pension plan. The taxman will add £2,580 in basic-rate tax relief and, hey presto, she has £12,900 sitting in her pension plan, just like Penny.

However, as a higher-rate taxpayer, Isabella will also receive higher-rate tax relief when she submits her tax return. To calculate this we simply multiply her gross pension contribution by 20%:

$$£12,900 \times 20\% = £2,580$$

In summary, Penny and Isabella have both saved exactly the same amount of money but because Isabella waited until she became a higher-rate taxpayer before making pension contributions she ends up with £2,580 more than Penny.

Maximising the Pension Pot

In the above example Isabella has the same amount of money as Penny in her pension plus a tax refund from HMRC. However, if Isabella would prefer to maximise her pension savings she could do things slightly differently.

What she could do is make a bigger pension contribution – £13,760 instead of just her £10,320 ISA savings. The taxman will top this up with £3,440 to produce a gross pension contribution of £17,200.

Isabella won't be out of pocket despite making a bigger contribution because she will also receive a tax refund of £3,440 (£17,200 x 20%) – her higher-rate relief.

This means her total personal investment will simply be the amount she saved up in her ISA:

£13,760 pension contribution *minus* £3,440 tax refund = £10,320

Now look at the size of Isabella's pension pot. She has £17,200 compared with Penny's £12,900 – 33% more money!

33% – The Magic Number

The same 33% increase in pension savings can be enjoyed by anyone who postpones making pension contributions while temporarily a basic-rate taxpayer.

Regardless of whether you postpone for one year, 10 years or any other time period, and regardless of whether you are making big or small pension contributions, the result is exactly the same:

Your pension pot will be 33% bigger

Finally, remember that, although Isabella postpones her pension contributions, she does NOT postpone saving. Note too that she invests in an ISA so that, like Penny, she does not miss out on tax-free growth.

Practical Pointers

- The assumption is that Isabella enjoys the maximum higher-rate tax relief on her £17,200 pension contribution. However, we know from Chapter 4 that Isabella will only enjoy full higher-rate tax relief if she also has at least £17,200 of income taxed at 40%. If she doesn't, she may have to spread her pension contributions over more than one tax year.

- Isabella personally contributes £13,760, which is more than her £10,320 ISA savings. However, when she gets her tax refund back she is not left out of pocket. How do we calculate the number £13,760? Simply divide £10,320 by 0.75 to add on the higher-rate tax relief.

Chapter 18

Higher-Rate Taxpayers: Can They Put Off Pension Saving?

In the previous chapter I showed how basic-rate taxpayers may be better off postponing pension contributions until they become higher-rate taxpayers. What about higher-rate taxpayers – can they also put off making pension contributions?

Be careful about asking a financial advisor this question by the way. It's like giving Superman Kryptonite. They usually advise people to start making pension contributions as soon as possible. However, as I pointed out in the previous chapter, it's important to not confuse the benefits of saving in a pension with the benefits of saving *generally*.

There are lots of reasons why you might not feel like putting money into a pension right now, even though you would receive lots of tax relief. It all revolves around the lengthy jail sentence placed on pension savings – you can't access them until you are age 55 or older.

If you have big financial commitments, for example a mortgage or children's education to pay for many years, you may be very reluctant to tie up your savings in a pension.

You certainly shouldn't be making any pension contributions if you are in imminent danger of losing a big chunk or all of your income, for example if your business is struggling or you are worried about losing your job.

Am I saying it's not necessary to save in these situations? No, I'm a big fan of saving from day one. What I am saying is that you don't necessarily have to save via a pension... not at certain stages of your life at least. It's a fat lot of good having £100,000 in your pension pot if your home is about to be repossessed.

Before making any pension contributions, you should always make sure you have a significant amount of money saved elsewhere to protect against:

- An unforeseen drop in income, and
- Unforeseen expenses

But what about all the tax savings enjoyed by pension savers? If you delay putting money into a pension, won't you lose out? This is one of the great misconceptions about pensions.

As it happens, if you want immediate access to your savings, you don't have to put money into a pension until you are ready.

You will not be one penny worse off than someone who makes pension contributions continually for many years.

I've never heard any pension experts make this crucial point. Maybe it's because advising people to put off making pension contributions is bad for business, a bit like a tobacco company telling you to quit smoking.

Case Study – Postponing Pension Contributions

In Chapter 15 we compared Peter the pension saver with Ian the ISA investor. What we discovered is that pensions are much more powerful than traditional ISAs – you could end up with at least 41.67% more income from a pension.

However, it is possible that Ian, the ISA investor, will have the last laugh. Let's say he originally started saving into an ISA because he wanted access to his savings. Back then he was worried about losing his job and also had a big mortgage and three children to support. Move forward five years, his career's going well, the mortgage is smaller and the children have all flown the nest.

So he decides to take his ISA savings and stick them into a pension. Is he still worse off than Peter, who started saving in a pension five years earlier?

Table 5
Postponing Pension Contributions
Higher-Rate Taxpayers

End Year	Pension £	ISA £
1	10,700	6,420
2	22,149	13,289
3	34,399	20,640
4	47,507	28,504
5	61,533	36,920

Peter and Ian's savings up to the end of year five are summarised in Table 5. Just to recap, both are higher-rate taxpayers and both personally invest £6,000 per year. Peter enjoys income tax relief so his gross pension contribution is £10,000 per year, compared with Ian's £6,000 ISA investment. They both enjoy tax-free growth of 7% per year. After one year their £10,000 and £6,000 initial investments will be worth £10,700 and £6,420 respectively (explaining the first numbers you see in the table).

After five years Peter has £61,533, compared with Ian's £36,920. Ian now takes his ISA savings and sticks them in a pension. Because he knows he'll get a tax refund (his higher-rate tax relief) he actually makes an investment of £49,226 (£36,920/0.75). The taxman adds £12,307 of basic-rate tax relief and, hey presto, Ian ends up with £61,533 sitting in his pension pot – exactly the same as Peter!

Ian also gets a tax refund of £12,307 (£61,533 x 20%), so his £49,226 pension investment costs him just £36,920 personally – exactly the amount he accumulated in ISAs.

In summary, Peter started saving in a pension from day one, whereas Ian put his savings into an ISA, before transferring the money into a pension five years later. By postponing his pension contributions, Ian was able to access his savings in the event of a financial emergency. Postponing his contributions has not left him out of pocket.

Postponing Pension Contributions – The Dangers

I'm not encouraging anyone to postpone making pension contributions. The point of this exercise is to show that, all things being equal, there is *mathematically* no difference between regular pension contributions and a big catch-up pension contribution. Saving in a pension over many years will not leave you better off.

As with everything, compromise is often the best solution. There's nothing to stop you making some pension contributions now and further catch-up contributions when your personal financial situation is healthier.

There are also some dangers and some very important practical issues when it comes to postponing pension contributions:

Danger # 1 Higher Rate Tax Relief Could Be Scrapped

We discussed this danger in Chapter 6. For many years there have been fears that higher-rate tax relief on pension contributions will be scrapped because it costs the Government so much.

One option would be to give everyone the same flat rate of tax relief (such as 30%). Such a change would be more generous to basic-rate taxpayers but punish higher-rate taxpayers.

Alternatively, higher-rate tax relief could be kept but with the annual allowance reduced from £40,000 to, say, £30,000 or less.

Even if the current Conservative Government makes no changes to pension tax relief, there's nothing to stop a future government making the system less generous. Remember pensions are ultra long-term savings vehicles and your contributions will be made under multiple governments, possibly with widely differing views on tax.

Many higher-rate taxpayers may therefore feel that it is wise not to postpone making pension contributions and make hay while the sun is still shining, i.e. make pension contributions NOW while higher-rate tax relief is still available.

Danger # 2 Loss of Employer Pension Contributions

If you belong to a workplace pension scheme to which your employer is contributing, postponing your own contributions could prove costly: you will lose the free cash being offered by your employer (see Chapter 22).

Danger # 3 Your Earnings Fall

If your income falls and you are no longer a higher-rate taxpayer when the time comes to make catch-up contributions, you will not enjoy any higher-rate tax relief.

This could happen if you own a business that enters a long tough patch or period of decline. It could also happen to a company employee who suffers redundancy and is unable to find another job that pays well.

Danger # 4 Pension Recycling Rules

If you make larger than normal pension contributions a couple of years before you withdraw tax-free cash from your pension, there is a danger that HMRC will argue that you are recycling your tax-free lump sum.

If the recycling rules are triggered, your tax-free lump sum will be treated as an unauthorised payment, resulting in a tax charge of up to 70% (see Chapter 9).

According to HMRC, the recycling rules will also apply if, instead of funding the pension contribution directly from your tax-free lump sum, you use your available savings to pay the contribution and then use your tax-free lump sum to replenish those savings.

The recycling rules will be triggered if you always intended your tax-free lump sum to be an integral way of paying the increased pension contributions, albeit indirectly.

It's difficult to quantify the risk of triggering the recycling rules but the uncertainty alone is good enough reason to be careful of making bigger than normal pension contributions within a couple of years of withdrawing tax-free cash from your pension.

Practical Issue # 1 Maximising Higher Rate Tax Relief

Ian has to make a gross pension contribution of £61,533 to catch up with Peter. We know from Chapter 4 that to obtain the maximum higher-rate tax relief he must also have at least £61,533 of income taxed at 40%. Most people don't.

The bigger your catch-up contribution, the less likely you are to obtain the maximum higher-rate tax relief. Fortunately, there is a possible solution: Ian could spread his catch-up contributions over several tax years to maximise his higher-rate tax relief. This means he shouldn't leave it too close to retirement to make his catch-up contributions, especially if he has other savings he would like to put into a pension in addition to his ISA savings.

Practical Issue # 2 Exceeding the Annual Allowance

The bigger your catch-up contribution, the more likely you are to exceed the annual allowance (see Chapter 2). The annual allowance is currently £40,000 and could be reduced in the years ahead.

Fortunately, it is possible to carry forward any unused annual allowance from the three previous tax years, so a gross pension contribution of up to £160,000 is allowed in 2020/21, provided you have sufficient relevant UK earnings and belonged to a pension scheme in each of those previous years.

Again, the best practical solution for Ian would probably be to spread his contributions over several tax years.

Practical Issue # 3 Tax Free Growth

Ian is able to catch up with Peter because he also enjoys tax-free investment growth in his ISA. If Ian's savings are taxed, he will end up permanently worse off, even after he puts his savings in a pension.

In summary, it is possible to put off pension saving if you don't want to tie up your money right now... but there are dangers and practical obstacles.

Chapter 19

How to Protect Your Child Benefit

Child benefit is an extremely valuable tax-free gift from the Government to parents. Those who qualify currently receive the following annual payments:

- £1,094.60   for the first child
- £725.40   for each subsequent child

Depending on the number of children, a family can expect to receive the following total child benefit payment:

Children	Total Child Benefit
1	£1,095
2	£1,820
3	£2,545
4	£3,271

plus £725.40 for each additional child

You can keep receiving child benefit until your children are 16 years of age or until age 20 if they are enrolled in 'relevant education' (the likes of GCSEs, A Levels, and NVQs to level 3, but not degree courses).

That's the good news. The bad news is the Government withdraws the benefit where any member of the household has annual income in excess of £50,000.

The withdrawal operates by levying an income tax charge on the *highest earner* in the household.

How the Child Benefit Charge Works

For every £100 the highest earner's income exceeds £50,000, there is a tax charge equivalent to 1% of the child benefit. So if the highest earner in the household has an income of £51,000, the tax charge is 10% of the child benefit.

For a household with two children this means a tax charge of £182 (£1,820 x 10%).

If the highest earner has an income of £55,000, the tax charge is 50% of the child benefit. For a household with two children this means a tax charge of £910.

Once the highest earner's income reaches £60,000, all the child benefit will effectively have been withdrawn.

As an alternative to the income tax charge, the claimant can choose not to receive child benefit.

1970s Style Tax Rates

The child benefit charge creates some truly eye-watering marginal tax rates for some parents with income between £50,000 and £60,000.

For example, let's say the highest earner's taxable income goes up from £50,000 to £51,000.

They will pay £400 more income tax and a 10% child benefit charge – £109 for a household with one child. So the total tax charge on the additional £1,000 is £509 – that's a marginal tax rate of 51%!

And if you think that's bad, take a look at the marginal tax rates suffered by parents with more than one child:

2 Children   58%
3 Children   65%
4 Children   73%

You can add an extra 2% to all of the above tax rates to take account of national insurance, if your income is from employment or self-employment. The marginal tax rates for dividends are different.

Not all Income is Equal

The child benefit charge only applies if your 'adjusted net income' is over £50,000.

Adjusted net income includes all income subject to income tax, including employment income, profits from self employment, pensions and income from property, savings and dividends.

Income from tax-free investments like ISAs is excluded. What this means is that a parent with work-related income of £50,000 and tax-free dividends of £10,000 from an ISA will avoid the child benefit charge completely; someone with the same £50,000 of earned income but £10,000 of rental income will effectively lose all of their child benefit.

This makes investments like shares and bonds (that can be sheltered inside an ISA) potentially far more tax efficient than rental property.

For example, that £10,000 in rental income will produce an income tax bill of £4,000 and a child benefit charge of £1,820 for a family with two children. Total rental income net of all taxes is just £4,180.

The ISA investor ends up with 139% more income!

How Pension Contributions Can Help

One of the simplest ways for almost all taxpayers to avoid the child benefit charge is by making pension contributions. This is because your adjusted net income is reduced by your gross pension contributions.

In Chapter 18 we looked at the pros and cons of postponing pension contributions if you are a higher-rate taxpayer. Those in the £50,000-£60,000 income bracket, who are the highest earners in households in receipt of child benefit, should be very wary of postponing pension contributions.

By making pension contributions they can enjoy above average levels of tax relief. Let's take a look at some of the potential tax savings:

Example

Alan has taxable income of £55,000. His wife earns £30,000 and claims child benefit for three children: £2,545. On the top £5,000 slice of his income, Alan faces a £2,000 income tax bill and a child benefit charge of £1,272 (50% of the family's child benefit, rounded down to the nearest whole pound). Alan's £5,000 is reduced to just £1,728.

Let's focus in on that top £5,000 slice of his income and see how he can protect himself from the child benefit charge:

Alan personally contributes £4,000 into his pension. The taxman adds £1,000 of basic-rate tax relief, producing a gross pension contribution of £5,000. When Alan submits his tax return he also receives £1,000 of higher-rate tax relief (£5,000 x 20%).

Furthermore, because Alan's adjusted net income has fallen to £50,000, he escapes the £1,272 child benefit charge.

Alan enjoys a total of £3,272 tax relief on his £5,000 pension contribution, i.e. 65% tax relief.

He ends up with £5,000 in his pension pot instead of £1,728 in after-tax income.

What this example shows is that many parents in the £50,000-£60,000 bracket will enjoy tax relief on their pension contributions of 58% (two children), 65% (three children) or maybe even more, compared with the 40% tax relief enjoyed by most other higher-rate taxpayers.

Bigger than Normal Pension Contributions

Those in the £50,000-£60,000 income bracket should consider making bigger than normal pension contributions, in particular if they expect their income to rise above £60,000 in the future or if their children are approaching the age where child benefit will be withdrawn.

Example

Gordon has taxable income of £60,000 in 2020/21. His wife earns £30,000 and claims child benefit for two children: £1,820. On the top £10,000 slice of his income, Gordon faces a 58% tax charge: £4,000 income tax and a child benefit charge of £1,820.

Gordon wouldn't normally make a gross pension contribution of more than £5,000 but decides to double his contribution for the current tax year so that he can take advantage of the 58% tax relief available (two children).

He could then suspend making any pension contributions in 2021/22, for example if his income rises from £60,000 to £65,000. A £5,000 pension contribution in 2021/22 would attract just 40% tax relief, compared with the 58% available in 2020/21.

Much Bigger than Normal Pension Contributions

Even those with income *over* £60,000 can enjoy above average levels of tax relief by making bigger than normal pension contributions.

Example
Colin has taxable income of £65,000 in 2020/21. His wife earns £30,000 and receives child benefit for three children: £2,545. On the top £15,000 slice of his income, Colin faces an £8,545 tax charge: £6,000 income tax and a £2,545 child benefit charge.

If Colin makes a gross pension contribution of £5,000 he will enjoy 40% tax relief, just like most other higher-rate taxpayers. He will not avoid any of the child benefit charge because his adjusted net income will not fall below £60,000.

Fortunately his aunt Doris left him some money so Colin decides to make a much bigger than normal £15,000 gross pension contribution in 2020/21 and then stop making contributions for a year or two.

Colin's pension contribution attracts £6,000 income tax relief and, by reducing his adjusted net income to £50,000, allows him to entirely avoid the £2,545 child benefit charge. The total tax relief is £8,545 or 57% of his gross pension contribution.

Obviously the higher your income the bigger the pension contribution you have to make to get your income below £60,000 and ultimately down to £50,000. However, for some individuals, including those with income well over £60,000, the tax relief may make it worthwhile.

The key tax planning point is that you shouldn't necessarily think in terms of avoiding the child benefit charge completely or permanently.

For those with income close to £60,000 (or over £60,000 in some cases) it may be more practical to think in terms of reducing only part of the charge or reducing it in some tax years but not others.

Postponing Pension Contributions

In Chapter 17 I argued that some basic-rate taxpayers should consider postponing pension contributions until their income rises above £50,000 and they become higher-rate taxpayers.

With the child benefit charge also kicking in at this income level, this is another reason to consider postponing contributions until your income rises above £50,000. You could then make bigger than normal catch-up contributions which enjoy more tax relief.

In Scotland the higher-rate threshold kicks in when your income goes above £43,430, so some higher-rate taxpayers in Scotland may wish to consider postponing pension contributions until their income rises above £50,000.

Couples Pension Planning

Where one spouse or partner is in the £50,000-£60,000 income bracket and the other has a smaller income, it may be worth getting the higher earner to make most of the family's pension contributions, even for just one or two tax years.

Example
Chris and Maria earn £60,000 and £50,000 respectively. They receive child benefit for two children: £1,820. In recent years they've been making pension contributions of £5,000 each. In 2020/21 the couple decide that Maria should stop her pension contributions and Chris should increase his by £5,000 to £10,000. By making an additional £5,000 pension contribution Chris will avoid an additional 50% child benefit charge, saving the couple £910. Furthermore, with the higher-rate threshold currently £50,000, Maria would not enjoy any higher-rate tax relief on any pension contribution she makes. Chris will enjoy the maximum higher-rate tax relief.

Both Individuals Earn £50,000-£60,000

Where both income earners in the household are in the £50,000-£60,000 bracket, the most tax-efficient strategy is to *equalise* their adjusted net incomes.

Example
Alistair earns £58,000, his wife Wilma earns £55,000. The couple want to make a £5,000 gross pension contribution in 2020/21. If Alistair makes the entire contribution this will take his adjusted net income to £53,000. Wilma will then become the household's highest earner with £55,000, resulting in a 50% child benefit charge.

The best solution may be for Alistair to make a £4,000 gross pension contribution, with Wilma making a £1,000 gross contribution. They will both then have adjusted net income of £54,000 and an additional 10% of their child benefit will be retained.

The Self-Employed

The taxable income of self-employed individuals (sole traders and business partners) tends to fluctuate more than that of salaried employees and even company owners.

A self-employed individual's taxable income is essentially the pre-tax profits of the business. These will vary from year to year if business conditions improve or decline or if the business owner alters the level of tax deductible spending (e.g. by making investments in tax deductible equipment or vehicles).

As a result some self-employed business owners, who are also parents of qualifying children, may find themselves in the £50,000-£60,000 income bracket in some tax years but not others.

Where possible they should consider always making pension contributions in those '£50,000-£60,000' tax years, possibly contributions that are bigger than normal.

Other Considerations & Drawbacks

To maximise the tax relief on pension contributions it may be necessary to postpone or bring forward contributions or have one household member make bigger contributions than another.

Actions like these may have other consequences that need to be considered. For example, the second member of the household may not be happy about the highest earner accumulating all the retirement savings!

Postponing pension contributions may not be a good idea if this means you forfeit contributions from your employer (see Chapter 22) or if higher-rate tax relief is eventually abolished (see Chapter 6).

Chapter 20

Higher Income Earners

Income between £100,000 and £125,000

Once your income exceeds £100,000 your income tax personal allowance is gradually taken away. It is reduced by £1 for every £2 you earn above £100,000.

For example, if your income is £110,000 your personal allowance will be reduced by £5,000.

The income tax personal allowance for the 2020/21 tax year is £12,500. So once your income reaches £125,000 you will have no personal allowance at all.

This is a real tax sting for those earning over £100,000. The personal allowance currently saves you £5,000 in tax if you are a higher-rate taxpayer.

Paying Tax at 60%

The effect of having your personal allowance taken away is that anyone earning between £100,000 and £125,000 faces a hefty marginal income tax rate of 60%.

For example, someone who earns £100,000 and receives an extra £10,000 will pay 40% tax on the extra income – £4,000.

They'll also have their personal allowance reduced by £5,000, which means they'll have to pay an extra £2,000 in tax (£5,000 x 40%). Total tax on extra income: £6,000 which is 60%.

Saving Tax at 60%

The flipside of this is that anyone in this income bracket who makes pension contributions can currently enjoy 60% tax relief.

Your personal allowance is reduced if your 'adjusted net income' is more than £100,000. When calculating your adjusted net income you usually deduct any pension contributions you have made.

For example, let's say you have taxable income of £110,000 and invest £8,000 in a pension. For starters you will receive a £2,000 top up from the taxman (your basic-rate tax relief), resulting in a gross pension contribution of £10,000. You'll also receive higher-rate tax relief of £2,000 (£10,000 x 20%).

In addition, by making a gross pension of £10,000 your 'adjusted net income' will be reduced from £110,000 to £100,000, so none of your personal allowance will be taken away. Additional tax saving: £2,000 (£5,000 x 40%).

In summary, your £10,000 pension contribution produces £6,000 of tax savings – a total of 60% tax relief!

Income over £125,000

Once your income rises above £125,000 your marginal income tax rate falls back to 40%. However, making quite big pension contributions can still be attractive because you may still get 60% tax relief on some of the money you put away.

For example, let's say you have taxable income of £135,000 and put £28,000 into a pension. Like anyone else you will receive £7,000 basic-rate tax relief, resulting in a gross pension contribution of £35,000. And like any other higher-rate taxpayer you will receive an additional £7,000 of higher-rate relief (£35,000 x 20%).

In addition, your £35,000 gross pension contribution will reduce your adjusted net income from £135,000 to £100,000, so none of your personal allowance will be taken away. Additional tax saving: £5,000 (£12,500 x 40%).

In summary, your £35,000 gross pension contribution produces £19,000 of tax savings – a total of 54% tax relief.

In fact, anyone with taxable income up to £150,000 will enjoy *at least* 50% tax relief by making a gross pension contribution that's big enough to take their adjusted net income back down to £100,000.

For example, someone with taxable income of £150,000 would need to make a gross pension contribution of £50,000 to take their adjusted net income back down to £100,000 and enjoy exactly 50% tax relief.

Although the tax relief is attractive, that's a big pension contribution, so in practice this strategy may appeal most to those whose income is only slightly higher than the £125,000 threshold.

Furthermore, pension contributions in excess of £40,000 will exceed the annual allowance and are only possible if you have unused annual allowance from the three previous tax years.

The Tapered Annual Allowance

When your income rises above £150,000 you become an additional-rate taxpayer and start paying tax at 45% on most types of income. The flipside is you can enjoy 45% tax relief on your pension contributions.

However, some additional-rate taxpayers face greater restrictions to their pension contributions than other taxpayers. The annual allowance – the maximum amount that can be invested in a pension each year – can be reduced from £40,000 to just £4,000.

Fortunately, following an announcement in the March 2020 Budget, this pension taper now only kicks in at much higher income levels than previously. As a result, many high earners can benefit from much higher pension contributions than before.

Threshold Income

The first thing you have to calculate is your 'threshold income'. If your threshold income is £200,000 or less you are completely exempt from tapering and can make pension contributions just like anyone else.

Your threshold income is, broadly speaking, your total taxable income. This includes your salary, self-employment profits, dividends, rental profits, interest income and any other taxable income you receive.

From this you deduct any pension contributions you have made *personally* (you deduct the gross contributions).

You can also deduct other reliefs listed in Section 24 of the Income Tax Act 2007. These include things like trade loss relief.

Employer pension contributions are ignored when calculating threshold income. But you must add back any salary sacrificed in exchange for employer pension contributions since 9 July 2015.

The threshold used to be £110,000 but was increased to £200,000 in the March 2020 Budget. It applies from 6 April 2020.

Example 1

Dirk is self-employed and has taxable income of £225,000 this year (made up mostly of his profits from self-employment and a portfolio of rental properties). He makes a gross pension contribution of £40,000 into his SIPP (he invests £32,000 personally and the taxman tops this up with £8,000).

His gross pension contribution is deducted from his taxable income, giving him a threshold income of £185,000. Because Dirk's threshold income is less than £200,000, he is completely unaffected by the tapered annual allowance. This means his annual allowance for the current tax year (his permitted pension contribution) is £40,000.

Example 2

Beric is a company owner and pays himself salary and dividend income totalling £200,000. He also has taxable rental profits of £40,000, so his total taxable income is £240,000.

His company makes a pension contribution of £35,000 on his behalf (an employer pension contribution) but we ignore this when calculating his threshold income. He doesn't make any pension contributions personally.

Beric's threshold income is therefore £240,000. Because this exceeds £200,000, he is potentially affected by the tapered annual allowance.

Adjusted Income

If your threshold income exceeds £200,000 the next thing you have to calculate is your 'adjusted income'. Broadly speaking, your adjusted income is your total taxable income *plus* any pension contributions made by your employer.

You also add back any contributions to an occupational pension scheme under a net pay arrangement (where your contributions are deducted from your salary before calculating PAYE).

You can also deduct the reliefs listed in Section 24 of the Income Tax Act 2007.

Your annual allowance will only be reduced if your adjusted income exceeds £240,000 (previously £150,000). The annual allowance is reduced by £1 for every £2 your adjusted income exceeds £240,000. So an individual with adjusted income of £270,000 will have their annual allowance reduced by £15,000 (£30,000/2), giving them an annual allowance of £25,000.

The annual allowance cannot fall below £4,000.

Pension contributions that exceed the tapered annual allowance face the annual allowance charge. The excess contributions will be added to your income and taxed. If the charge exceeds £2,000 it may be possible to have it paid out of your pension savings. This may only be possible if total contributions to the scheme in question exceed the standard annual allowance (£40,000).

Example 2 continued
As we saw earlier, Beric has total taxable income of £240,000 and his company makes a contribution of £35,000 on his behalf.

Beric's adjusted income is £275,000 (£240,000 + £35,000)

His annual allowance is cut by (£275,000 - £240,000)/2 = £17,500

His annual allowance is therefore £40,000 - £17,500 = £22,500

Beric faces an annual allowance charge on £12,500:

£35,000 - £22,500 = £12,500

Calculating the Tapered Annual Allowance in Practice

Beric can avoid the charge by getting his company to make a smaller pension contribution (no more than £26,667).

Alternatively, he may be able to extract less income from his company (no more than £215,000) to benefit from a tapered annual allowance of £35,000. Company owners will find it easier than others to control their taxable income to reduce their threshold income and adjusted income. But they may have to be wary of triggering a special tax anti-avoidance rule (see below).

Most regular salaried employees will find it fairly easy to calculate their adjusted income and threshold income. So too will company owners who pay themselves a set amount of salary and dividend income. Problems may arise where the taxpayer has income that is less predictable, for example profits from self employment or rental profits from property. In these circumstances it may not be possible to calculate how much taxable income you have (and thus the tapered annual allowance) until *after* the tax year has ended. By then it will be too late to make pension contributions.

Those who wish to benefit from pension contributions and think they are affected by the tapered annual allowance may therefore need to estimate their total taxable income just *before* the end of the tax year.

The Tapered Annual Allowance and Carry Forward

Fortunately, all is not lost if your pension contributions exceed your tapered annual allowance for the year. Those affected by the tapered annual allowance can still carry forward any unused annual allowance from the three previous tax years. For example, if your annual allowance this year is reduced from £40,000 to £30,000 and you make a £20,000 pension contribution, you will have £10,000 left to carry forward to next year (£30,000 - £20,000).

Carry forward could act as a lifeline for those whose pension contributions accidentally exceed the tapered annual allowance in any given year. Beric in the above example will avoid the annual allowance charge if he has at least £12,500 of unused annual allowance from the three previous tax years.

Anti-Avoidance Rule

An anti-avoidance rule is in place to prevent anyone entering into an arrangement which involves reducing their adjusted or threshold income and increasing their income in a different tax year. The anti-avoidance provisions apply when it is reasonable to assume that the main purpose, or one of the main purposes of the arrangement, is to reduce the impact of the tapered annual allowance. If the anti-avoidance provisions apply, then the relevant arrangement will be ignored for the purposes of calculating the tapered annual allowance.

It is unclear how this anti-avoidance rule could be applied to individuals such as company owners who vary their income from year to year.

Maximum Pension Contribution

Thanks to the change announced in the March 2020 Budget many additional-rate taxpayers are now unaffected by the tapered annual allowance and can once again make fairly big pension contributions with full tax relief.

For example, anyone with a taxable income of up to £240,000 can personally contribute up to £40,000 to a pension every year (assuming there are no employer contributions). The following table shows how much high earners can personally contribute at different income levels.

Taxable income	Maximum pension contribution*
Up to £240,000	£40,000
£250,000	£35,000
£260,000	£30,000
£270,000	£25,000
£280,000	£20,000
£290,000	£15,000
£300,000	£10,000
£310,000	£5,000
£312,000	£4,000

* Maximum gross contribution that can be paid personally. Assumes there is no employer contribution. Ignores carry forward from 3 previous tax years.

Maximum Contributions – Company Owners

A company owner with taxable income of up to £200,000 can get their company to make a pension contribution of up to £40,000 every year with full tax relief.

The following table shows how much the company can contribute at different income levels:

Taxable Income	Maximum Company Pension Contribution*
Up to £200,000	£40,000
£215,000	£35,000
£230,000	£30,000
£245,000	£25,000
£260,000	£20,000
£275,000	£15,000
£290,000	£10,000
£305,000	£5,000
£308,000+	£4,000

* Assumes there is no contribution by the company owner personally. Ignores potential carry forward from 3 previous tax years

Planning under the Tapered Annual Allowance

Some very high income earners may be comfortable with a reduced annual allowance. For example, a sole trader with profits of £260,000, who makes regular pension contributions of £20,000 per year, may be quite happy with an annual allowance of £30,000.

However, if they expect their income to increase, resulting in further reductions in their annual allowance, it may be desirable for them to make bigger pension contributions now while they can. In other words, it may be better to contribute £30,000 now instead of £20,000.

Some individuals whose threshold income is *below* £200,000 at present may also wish to speed up their pension contributions at present if they expect to be earning well over £200,000 in a few years' time.

It may also be possible to mitigate the damage caused by the tapered annual allowance by getting your spouse to make bigger pension contributions, even if these only attract 40% tax relief.

Example
Miriam is a self-employed solicitor with profits of £300,000 and her husband Nick earns £100,000. During the current tax year Miriam would like to make a pension contribution of £40,000 but is restricted to £10,000. Nick normally makes pension contributions of £10,000 per year.

The couple therefore decide to swap the amounts they contribute: Nick contributes £40,000 per year (using the couple's shared resources) and Miriam contributes £10,000.

Nick's additional pension contribution of £30,000 will only attract 40% tax relief, compared with Miriam's 45%, however the total loss of tax relief is just £1,500 (£30,000 x 5%).

For this strategy to work it is essential that Nick has sufficient income taxed at 40% so that all of the additional contribution attracts higher-rate tax relief (see Chapter 4).

It may also be essential that Nick's higher contributions do not result in him building such a big pension pot that his withdrawals, when he eventually retires, are taxed at 40% instead of 20%.

Part 5

Employees

Chapter 21

Auto-Enrolment: The Advent of Compulsory Pensions

"Currently 14 million people get no contribution from their employer towards a pension."

Former Secretary of State for Work and Pensions, Yvette Cooper, January 2010

To address this problem, compulsory workplace pensions have been phased in over the last few years. Known as 'auto enrolment' it forces all employers to enrol nearly all their staff into a workplace pension.

Exemptions

Only employees earning more than £10,000 and aged from 22 to state pension age need to be *automatically* enrolled into a pension. However, some older and younger employees and those who earn less than £10,000 also have workplace pension rights:

- If an employee earns less than £6,240 in 2020/21 they don't need to be automatically enrolled but the employer has to give them access to a pension if they request it and if they are aged between 16 and 74. However, the employer is not required to contribute.

- If an employee earns between £6,240 and £10,000 and their age is between 16 and 74 they don't need to be automatically enrolled but do have the right to opt in. If they do decide to join the pension scheme the employer will have to contribute as well.

- If an employee earns more than £10,000 but is aged 16-21 or between state pension age and 74 they don't need to be automatically enrolled but do have the right to opt in. If they do decide to join the pension scheme the employer will have to contribute as well.

Company Directors

According to the Pension Regulator a company does not have any automatic-enrolment duties when:

- It has just one director, with no other staff

- It has a number of directors, none of whom has an employment contract, with no other staff

- It has a number of directors, only one of whom has an employment contract, with no other staff

A contract of employment does not have to be in writing. However, according to the Pension Regulator, if there is no written contract of employment, or other evidence of an intention to create an employer/worker relationship between the company and the director, it will not argue that an employment contract exists.

If a director does not have an employment contract they are always exempt from automatic enrolment.

If a director has a contract of employment and there are other people working for the company with an employment contract, they are not exempt.

Depending on their age and earnings, they may qualify for automatic enrolment but the company can decide whether to automatically enrol them into a pension.

However, the director has the right to join a pension scheme at any time and the company cannot refuse to enrol them (although in practice this problem will not arise in most owner-managed companies).

If the company decides not to enrol any employed director who is eligible for automatic enrolment, and it has no other eligible staff, it does not need to set up a pension scheme.

However, it will still need to make a 'declaration of compliance'.

The Contributions

Employers are forced to make a minimum pension contribution and, in practice, so too are most employees.

Generally speaking, contributions are a percentage of 'qualifying earnings'.

From 6 April 2019 onwards the total minimum contribution is 8% with at least 3% coming from the employer.

The total minimum contribution can be paid by the employer but in practice many small firms will insist that the employee makes up the required balance.

This means that from 6 April 2019 onwards many employees will be forced to contribute 5% to a pension if they want to benefit from a 3% contribution from their employer.

Employees' contributions enjoy tax relief as normal, which means 4% will come from them personally and the extra 1% will be added by the taxman in the form of basic-rate tax relief.

Qualifying Earnings

The minimum contributions are generally not based on the employee's total earnings but rather on a band of earnings.

The lower and upper thresholds for 2020/21 are £6,240 and £50,000 respectively. What this means is that pension contributions are typically based on earnings of up to £43,760 (£50,000 - £6,240).

For example, someone with employment income of £60,000 will have their pension contributions based on earnings of £43,760. Someone with employment income of £20,000 will have their pension contributions based on earnings of £13,760 (£20,000 - £6,240).

Opting out

Employees will be automatically enrolled but can opt out if they wish by completing an opt-out notice. Employers are, however, required to automatically re-enrol eligible employees back into the workplace pension scheme roughly every three years.

No doubt some employees, especially younger employees, will prefer to opt out if they are compelled by their employers to make a pension contribution of up to 5%.

How Valuable is Auto Enrolment?

The answer to this question probably depends on whether you are an employee or employer.

Many small business owners cannot afford to save for their own retirement, let alone those of their entire workforce!

And this, perhaps, is the crucial point. If your employer has been dragged kicking and screaming into a system of compulsory pensions, you may end up being paid less to cover the cost. For example, future pay increases may be reduced. This is basic economics.

Even an 8% pension contribution is not big enough to solve most people's retirement saving problem, especially since it will typically be based on a small band of the employee's earnings.

For example, let's say you currently earn £65,000 and you and your employer make a combined 8% pension contribution for 20 years (based on the £43,760 band of qualifying earnings), with all amounts increased to take account of inflation.

After 20 years the pension pot will be worth around £179,000, if the investments in the fund grow by, say, 7% per year. That's a tidy sum BUT insignificant in terms of providing you with a meaningful retirement income.

In 20 years' time your salary will have grown to around £95,000, so the money paid into your pension pot will be worth less than two years' salary – not exactly enough for a golden retirement!

This does not mean that you should opt out of auto-enrolment. That would mean forfeiting the pension contribution your employer makes, which could arguably be regarded as free money.

What it does mean is that those who are making the minimum pension contribution under auto enrolment will almost certainly need to build additional retirement savings, either using pensions or other savings products.

Chapter 22

Free Cash from Employers

As we know from the previous chapter, many individuals enjoy more than just tax relief on their pension contributions. They also receive 'free' money from their employers.

Many company pension schemes offer far more generous employer contributions than those required under the auto-enrolment rules. Some employees receive employer contributions totalling 5%-10% of their salary, provided they contribute a similar amount. With the help of employer pension contributions, you may be able to save twice as quickly as you could on your own.

Sometimes employers will double what you put in. For example, in one pension scheme I know about, the company puts in 12% if the employee puts in 6%.

Many employees recognize that giving up any of this free money (by not contributing at all or not contributing enough) is tantamount to looking a gift horse in the mouth.

I remember listening on the radio to a woman describe how she and her husband were trying to cut out every single bit of frivolous spending so that they could contribute as much as possible to her husband's workplace pension scheme, thereby enjoying a hefty matching contribution from the employer.

She described it as "austerity today for prosperity tomorrow".

Not everyone has been as financially prudent as this couple. According to Standard Life, before the advent of auto-enrolment employers were offering a contribution to around 10 million employees but around 4.5 million did not sign up to their employer's pension scheme.

These employees were missing out on a total of nearly £6 billion per year of free money!

Not surprisingly in the past it has been younger employees who have contributed the least to pensions. According to the

Department for Work and Pensions, in 2011 only 15% of employees aged 16-24 participated in workplace pension schemes, whereas pension participation was 58% in the 45-54 age group.

Millions more people now belong to a workplace pension thanks to the introduction of compulsory pensions (see Chapter 21) BUT some employees (e.g. younger employees) may opt out.

I'm not in the business of criticising the savings habits of others, especially those who have children to support. Many families have very little income left after paying extortionate amounts of income tax, national insurance and VAT and after paying down debts like student loans and home mortgages.

Nevertheless, if there is ever a good time to contribute to a pension it's when your employer is offering you money on a plate.

Example
Douglas is an employee with a salary of £60,000 per year. Let's say his employer offers to make a 5% pension contribution, with Douglas contributing 5% personally.

If Douglas decides to opt out of his workplace pension scheme, he will have additional income of £3,000 (£60,000 x 5%). After paying income tax he will be left with £1,800.

Alternatively, if Douglas decides to join his workplace pension scheme he will end up with £6,000 sitting in his pension (£3,000 contributed personally and £3,000 from his employer).

Douglas has to decide whether £1,800 of income today is more valuable than £6,000 tucked away until he retires.

This is just a snapshot from a single year. Douglas will lose £4,200 (£6,000 - £1,800) every year he is not a member of his employer's pension scheme. Furthermore, he will also lose the tax-free growth on that money. If a 25-year-old decides to forego a pension contribution from his employer he will lose possibly 40 years of tax-free compound growth. On next year's foregone contribution he will lose 39 years of tax-free growth... and so on.

So how much do you stand to lose over the long term by not receiving pension contributions from your employer?

Example continued

Let's say Douglas opts out of his workplace pension scheme for five years and therefore loses out on five years of employer contributions (at 5% of his salary).

We'll assume his salary increases by 3% per year, which means the contributions from his employer will also grow by 3% per year. We'll also assume the money in his pension grows by 7% per year tax free.

Douglas loses out on the following employer contributions over the five-year period: £3,000, £3,090, £3,183, £3,278 and £3,377. When you add tax-free compound growth at 7% per year, the total value of the employer pension contributions after five years is £19,523.

However, that's not the end of the story. Depending on how far away Douglas is from retirement he could lose out on tax-free growth on this money for possibly another 10, 20, 30 or even 40 years. For example, those five years' worth of contributions will be worth £27,382 after 10 years, £53,865 after 20 years, £105,960 after 30 years and £208,439 after 40 years.

Remember, all we are looking at here are the contributions that would be made by Douglas's employer (the 'free money'). We are ignoring the contributions that he would make personally and on which he would enjoy full income tax relief.

The top half of Table 6 shows exactly the same thing for a range of different starting salaries. In each case we assume the salary grows by 3% per year, the employer makes a 5% pension contribution for five years and the money grows by 7% per year tax free.

For example, if your salary is £30,000 now and you lose out on five years' worth of employer contributions and an additional 15 years of tax-free growth on that money, the total loss to your pension pot after 20 years will be £26,932.

The second half of the table shows exactly the same thing except this time we assume the employee is not a member of the workplace pension scheme for 10 years. For example, if your salary is £30,000 now and you lose out on 10 years' worth of employer contributions and an additional 10 years of tax-free growth on that money, the total loss to your pension pot after 20 years will be £49,193.

Table 6
5% Employer Pension Contribution
Long-term Value

Employer Contributions for 5 Years
Value after...

Starting Salary £	10 Years £	20 Years £	30 Years £	40 Years £
20,000	9127	17,955	35,320	69,480
30,000	13,691	26,932	52,980	104,220
40,000	18,255	35,910	70,640	138,959
50,000	22,818	44,887	88,300	173,699
60,000	27,382	53,865	105,960	208,439
70,000	31,946	62,842	123,620	243,179
80,000	36,509	71,820	141,280	277,919
90,000	41,073	80,797	158,940	312,659
100,000	45,637	89,774	176,600	347,399

Employer Contributions for 10 Years
Value after...

Starting Salary £	10 Years £	20 Years £	30 Years £	40 Years £
20,000	16,672	32,795	64,514	126,908
30,000	25,007	49,193	96,770	190,362
40,000	33,343	65,591	129,027	253,816
50,000	41,679	81,989	161,284	317,270
60,000	50,015	98,386	193,541	380,724
70,000	58,350	114,784	225,798	444,178
80,000	66,686	131,182	258,054	507,632
90,000	75,022	147,579	290,311	571,086
100,000	83,358	163,977	322,568	634,540

Different Employer Pension Contributions

Different employers pay different amounts into their employees' pensions.

To find out how much a bigger or smaller employer contribution is worth all you have to do is scale the numbers in Table 6 up or down.

For example, if the employer offers a 10% contribution you simply double the numbers. In this case Douglas, with a starting salary of £60,000 and no contributions for five years, will have lost £107,730 after 20 years (£53,865 x 2).

If the employer offers an 8% contribution you multiply the numbers by 1.6 (found by dividing 8 by 5).

If the employer offers a 3% contribution you multiply the numbers by 0.6 (found by dividing 3 by 5).

... and so on.

Putting Things in Perspective

The numbers in the table are quite large and imply that, by not belonging to a workplace pension scheme, and not receiving pension contributions from your employer, you may be losing a lot of free money.

However, it's important to put the figures in perspective. Let's say Douglas is 35 years old and 30 years away from retirement. By not receiving employer pension contributions for five years, his pension pot will have lost £105,960 of free money after 30 years.

However, by that time his salary will have grown to £141,394 (growing at just 3% per year). What this means is that not contributing to his employer's pension for five years has cost him around nine months' salary.

Is this a price worth paying? Only Douglas can answer that.

And what if Douglas is a high flier and his pay increases by more than inflation, as he climbs the corporate ladder?

If we assume his salary grows by 7% per year we find that after 30 years he is sitting on a salary of £426,855. And his pension pot will have lost out on £114,184 worth of employer contributions.

In total Douglas will have lost just over three months' pay by not receiving pension contributions from his employer for five years.

Personally, I am of the opinion that anyone offered free cash by their employer should grasp the opportunity with open arms.

BUT...

If you do not belong to your workplace pension scheme for just a few years, this may not have a significant effect on your income in retirement IF you expect your salary to grow rapidly, resulting in bigger employer pension contributions in later years.

Part 6

Salary Sacrifice Pensions

Chapter 23

Introduction to Salary Sacrifice Pensions

How would you like to increase your pension contributions by up to 34%, with the taxman footing the entire bill? It seems too good to be true but this result can be achieved if you stop making pension contributions *personally* and get your employer to make them all for you.

This set-up is known as salary sacrifice (also salary exchange or 'smart pensions') and is used by some of the country's biggest companies, universities and other organisations, including BT, Tesco and the BBC.

In my opinion, a salary sacrifice pension is the best tax-saving opportunity available to regular salaried employees.

So how does it work? Salary sacrifice is all about saving *national insurance*, on top of the income tax relief you already receive when you make pension contributions.

Most people only enjoy income tax relief when they contribute to a pension. The income tax relief is attractive but it's not the maximum amount of tax relief available. When an employee contributes personally to a pension plan there is no refund of all the national insurance paid by both the employee and the employer. As much as £258 of national insurance is paid by the employee and employer on £1,000 of salary.

With salary sacrifice arrangements, it is possible to put a stop to these national insurance payments because your employer makes your pension contributions for you.

Pension contributions paid by employers are exempt from national insurance.

The national insurance savings can then be added to your pension pot.

Sacrificing Salary, Not Income

Because the employer has to pay all the employee's pension contributions, the employee in return has to sacrifice some salary.

However, it's important to stress that the employee's net take-home pay does not fall – it remains exactly the same.

With salary sacrifice there is no extra cost for either the employee or the employer.

Clamp Down on Salary Sacrifice

The Government was concerned about the amount of money lost from salary sacrifice schemes. As a result, the income tax and employer's national insurance advantages of some salary sacrifice schemes have been removed.

However, employer pension contributions, employer-provided pensions advice, employer-supported childcare, cycle to work schemes and ultra low emission cars are not affected and continue to benefit from income tax and national insurance relief.

Company Pension Scheme Not Required

In theory salary sacrifice works with almost all pension plans including:

- Self-invested personal pensions (SIPPs)
- Personal pensions (group and individual plans)
- Stakeholder pensions (group and individual plans)
- Occupational pension schemes

The main consideration for salary sacrifice purposes is that the plan must be able to accept employer contributions. Many SIPP providers have special forms for this purpose.

However, if a salary sacrifice pension arrangement is used by your employer in conjunction with his auto-enrolment duties, it's essential the pension plan is a "qualifying scheme" for auto-enrolment purposes.

The pension provider will be able to tell you if the scheme is qualifying or not.

Salary sacrifice can be used by most employees. However, sole traders and other self-employed individuals cannot use salary sacrifice because there is no employer to make pension contributions on their behalf.

There has to be an employer/employee relationship for a salary sacrifice arrangement to be successful.

Chapter 24

Income Tax & National Insurance: A Five-Minute Primer

There are several examples in the chapters that follow that use income tax and national insurance rates and allowances. In this chapter I'm going to briefly explain how income tax and national insurance are calculated for the average salary-earning employee. This should make the examples easier to understand (and slightly less painful!).

Calculating Income Tax

For the 2020/21 tax year, which started on 6 April 2020, most employees pay income tax as follows:

- 0%   on the first   £12,500   Personal allowance
- 20%   on the next   £37,500   Basic-rate band
- 40%   above   £50,000   Higher-rate threshold

If you earn more than £50,000 you are a higher-rate taxpayer; if you earn less you are a basic-rate taxpayer.

In Scotland you are a higher-rate taxpayer if you earn more than £43,430 and the rate is 41%. There's also a 19% 'starter rate' and a 21% 'intermediate rate'. The examples in the chapters that follow are based on the rates applying in the rest of the UK.

Example – Basic-Rate Taxpayer

John earns a salary of £25,000. His income tax for 2020/21 can be calculated as follows:

- *0% on the first £12,500 = £0*
- *20% on the next £12,500 = £2,500*

Total income tax bill: £2,500

Example – Higher-Rate Taxpayer

Jane earns a salary of £60,000. Her income tax for 2020/21 can be calculated as follows:

- *0% on the first £12,500 = £0*
- *20% on the next £37,500 = £7,500*
- *40% on the final £10,000 = £4,000*

Total income tax bill: £11,500

Income above £100,000 and £150,000

When your income exceeds £100,000 your tax-free personal allowance is gradually withdrawn and when your income exceeds £150,000 you also start paying tax at 45%.

Calculating National Insurance

For the 2020/21 tax year employees pay national insurance as follows:

- 0%   on the first £9,500   Primary threshold
- 12%   on the next £40,500
- 2%   above £50,000   Upper earnings limit

Employers generally pay 13.8% national insurance on every single pound the employee earns over £8,788. There is no cap.

You probably don't lose much sleep over your employer's national insurance bill. However, employer's national insurance is a tax on YOUR income. If it didn't exist your employer would be able to pay you a higher salary.

Here are John and Jane's national insurance calculations:

Example – Basic-Rate Taxpayer

John earns a salary of £25,000. His national insurance for 2020/21 can be calculated as follows:

- *0%   on the first   £9,500   = £0*
- *12%   on the next   £15,500   = £1,860*

John's national insurance bill: £1,860

John's employer pays national insurance on John's salary as follows:

- *0%   on the first   £8,788   = £0*
- *13.8% on the next   £16,212   = £2,237*

John's employer's national insurance bill: £2,237

Example – Higher-Rate Taxpayer

Jane earns a salary of £60,000. Her national insurance for 2020/21 can be calculated as follows:

- *0%   on the first   £9,500   = £0*
- *12%   on the next   £40,500   = £4,860*
- *2%   on the final £10,000   = £200*

Jane's national insurance bill: £5,060

Her employer's national insurance is:

- *0%   on the first   £8,788   = £0*
- *13.8% on the next   £51,212   = £7,067*

Jane's employer's national insurance bill: £7,067

Tax Bills Combined

John and Jane's tax bills can be summarised as follows:

John – Basic-rate Taxpayer – £25,000

	£
Income tax	2,500
Employee's national insurance	1,860
Employer's national insurance	2,237
Total taxes	**6,597**

Jane – Higher-rate Taxpayer – £60,000

	£
Income tax	11,500
Employee's national insurance	5,060
Employer's national insurance	7,067
Total taxes	**23,627**

When you include employer's national insurance it's startling how much tax is paid even by those on relatively modest incomes. Direct taxes on John's income come to 26%.

Jane's £60,000 salary is not low by any standards but you wouldn't describe her as a high income earner either. Nevertheless an amount equivalent to 39% of her salary is paid in direct taxes on her income.

Chapter 25

Salary Sacrifice Case Study: Basic-Rate Taxpayer

Introduction

We are going to follow the same John from the previous chapter and show how his own pension contributions can be increased by 34% with a salary sacrifice pension.

Remember John earns £25,000 and is a basic-rate taxpayer. Basic-rate taxpayers pay 20% income tax and 12% national insurance.

John's Retirement Savings

John pays income tax of £2,500 and national insurance of £1,860 on his £25,000 salary.

Let's say he also personally contributes £1,000 into his employer's pension scheme.

His employer pays the amount to the pension scheme provider who in turn reclaims £250 of basic-rate tax relief from HMRC and credits this to John's pension pot, bringing his total pension contribution to £1,250.

(The assumption here is that the pension scheme uses the 'relief at source' method rather than the 'net pay' method – see Chapter 2.)

The company John works for also makes an employer contribution into his pension plan. Although this is welcome, we will ignore this contribution and focus on John's own contributions.

After deducting his taxes and pension contribution he is left with a disposable income of £19,640.

Saving National Insurance

This is not a bad outcome but John can do much better. So far he has enjoyed full *income tax* relief on his pension contributions. However, income tax is not the only tax John pays. He also pays 12% national insurance on a significant chunk of his salary and his employer pays 13.8%.

Unfortunately, there is no national insurance relief for pension contributions made personally by employees like John. However, there is full national insurance relief for pension contributions made by employers.

John and his employer therefore agree that John will stop contributing personally to the pension scheme and his employer will make all the contributions for him. In return, John agrees to sacrifice some salary.

John's Salary Sacrifice

John sacrifices £1,470, which takes his salary from £25,000 to £23,530 (I explain why he sacrifices this amount later).

After deducting income tax and national insurance on £23,530 he is still left with £19,640 – the exact amount of disposable income he had before.

John's employer pays the £1,470 of sacrificed salary directly into John's pension plan.

His employer also contributes an additional £203, representing the employer's national insurance saving: £1,470 x 13.8% = £203. The amount going into John's pension pot now is £1,673 (plus his employer's original pre-salary sacrifice contribution).

In summary, John still has £19,640 of take-home pay, just as before, but his pension contribution has increased from £1,250 to £1,673 – an increase of 34%.

He is now saving 20% income tax, 12% employee's national insurance and 13.8% employer's national insurance on the money paid into his pension plan. A summary of the number crunching is contained on the next page.

John's Take Home Pay Stays the Same

	Before Salary Sacrifice	After Salary Sacrifice
	£	£
Salary	25,000	23,530
Less:		
Income tax	2,500	2,206
National insurance	1,860	1,684
Pension contribution	1,000	0
Disposable income	**19,640**	**19,640**

... But His Pension Contribution Increases By 34%

	Before Salary Sacrifice	After Salary Sacrifice
	£	£
Employee contribution	1,000	-
Taxman's top up	250	-
Extra employer contribution	-	1,470
Employer's NI saving paid in	-	203
Total	**1,250**	**1,673**

34% –The Magic Number!

Although this is just a one-year snapshot, what we can deduce from this simple example is that basic-rate taxpayers who use salary sacrifice can boost their pension contributions by 34%.

This means salary sacrifice could have a BIG impact on the amount of money you are able to save for retirement.

For example, if you would expect your own pension contributions to eventually grow in value to £100,000 without salary sacrifice, then you can expect them to grow to £134,000 with salary sacrifice.

If you would expect your own pension contributions to grow in value to £200,000 without salary sacrifice, then you can expect them to grow to £268,000 with salary sacrifice … and so on.

These are significant increases. Remember this extra money is completely **free**! You would not have to save a single penny extra to enjoy this boost to your retirement savings.

The extra money comes about because you and your employer are saving national insurance.

Note, your *total* pension pot will not increase by 34%, just the amount that you were originally contributing personally. Remember John's employer was already contributing to his pension before the salary sacrifice took place. His employer's *original* (pre-salary sacrifice) contributions will not increase under a salary sacrifice arrangement.

How to Calculate Your Own Salary Sacrifice

Let's say you are a basic-rate taxpayer and personally contribute £100 to a pension. To get that £100 you will have had to earn salary of £147:

£147 *less* 20% income tax *less* 12% national insurance = £100

So if you give up £147 of salary *and* stop making pension contributions you will still have almost exactly the same amount of disposable income.

Therefore, to calculate how much salary to sacrifice, while keeping your disposable income the same, you simply take your net pension contribution and add back the 20% income tax and 12% national insurance you have paid.

To do this quickly, divide your net pension contribution by 0.68:

$$\frac{\text{Net Pension Contribution}}{0.68}$$

Example 1

John, as we know, is a basic-rate taxpayer and personally contributes £1,000 to his employer's pension plan annually (this is his net pension contribution). His total gross contribution, including the taxman's top up, is £1,250. The amount of salary John needs to sacrifice is:

$$£1,000/0.68 = £1,470$$

If John stops contributing to his pension plan and sacrifices this amount of salary, his disposable income will remain the same.

His employer will contribute £1,470 to his pension plan plus an extra £203 (£1,470 x 13.8%), representing the employer's national insurance saving. His total pension contribution will be £1,673 – an increase of £423 per year or 34%.

Example 2

Richard is a basic-rate taxpayer and personally contributes £3,000 to his employer's pension plan annually (this is his net pension contribution). His total gross contribution, including the taxman's top up, is £3,750. The amount of salary Richard needs to sacrifice is calculated as follows:

$$£3,000/0.68 = £4,412$$

If Richard stops contributing to his pension plan and sacrifices this amount of salary, his disposable income will remain the same.

His employer will contribute £4,412 to his pension plan plus an extra £609 (£4,412 x 13.8%), representing the employer's national insurance saving. His total pension contribution will be £5,021 – an increase of £1,271 per year or 34%.

Chapter 26

Salary Sacrifice Case Study: Higher-Rate Taxpayer

Introduction

In this chapter we are going to follow the same Jane from Chapter 24 and show how she can boost her pension pot with a salary sacrifice arrangement.

Remember, Jane earns £60,000 and is a higher-rate taxpayer. Higher-rate taxpayers pay 40% income tax and 2% national insurance on their earnings over £50,000.

Jane's Retirement Savings

We know from Chapter 24 that Jane's income tax and national insurance bill comes to £16,560.

Let's say she also personally contributes £2,400 into her employer's pension scheme. Her employer pays the amount to the pension scheme provider who in turn reclaims £600 of basic-rate tax relief from HMRC and credits this to Jane's pension pot, bringing her total pension contribution to £3,000.

Jane also receives a £600 income tax refund when she submits her tax return (her higher-rate tax relief).

(The assumption here is that the pension scheme uses the 'relief at source' method rather than the 'net pay' method – see Chapter 2.)

The company Jane works for also makes an employer contribution into her pension plan. Although this is most welcome, we will ignore this contribution and focus on Jane's own contributions.

After deducting her taxes and pension contribution and adding back her higher-rate tax relief, Jane is left with disposable income of £41,640: £60,000 - £16,560 - £2,400 + £600.

Saving National Insurance

So far Jane has enjoyed full *income tax* relief on her pension contributions but no national insurance relief because, as we know, there is no national insurance relief for pension contributions made by employees.

So Jane decides to stop contributing personally and asks her employer to make the contributions directly. In return, Jane agrees to sacrifice £3,103 of salary which takes her from £60,000 to £56,897 – I'll explain why she sacrifices this exact amount shortly.

After deducting income tax and national insurance she is left with £41,640 – the exact amount of disposable income she had before.

Jane's employer pays the £3,103 of sacrificed salary directly into her pension plan. Her employer also contributes the employer's national insurance saving, which comes to £428 (£3,103 x 13.8%).

Jane's pension contribution is now £3,531 and has increased by 18%.

It's not as much as the 34% increase enjoyed by John, the basic-rate taxpayer, because higher-rate taxpayers generally only save 2% national insurance on the salary they sacrifice, whereas basic-rate taxpayers save 12%.

Both types of taxpayer, however, can benefit from their employers' 13.8% national insurance saving.

It is also important to remember that Jane is enjoying much more *income tax* relief than John (40% as opposed to 20%).

In summary, Jane is enjoying 40% income tax relief, 2% employee's national insurance relief and 13.8% employer's national insurance relief on the money she contributes to her pension plan.

A summary of the number crunching is contained on the next page.

Jane's Take Home Pay Stays the Same

	Before Salary Sacrifice	After Salary Sacrifice
	£	£
Salary	60,000	56,897
Less:		
Income tax	10,900*	10,259
National insurance	5,060	4,998
Pension contribution	2,400	0
Disposable income	**41,640**	**41,640**

... But Her Pension Contribution Increases By 18%

	Before Salary Sacrifice	After Salary Sacrifice
	£	£
Employee contribution	2,400	-
Taxman's top up	600	-
Extra employer contribution	-	3,103
Employer's NI saving	-	428
Total	**3,000**	**3,531**

* Reduced by £600 higher-rate income tax relief.

18% –The Magic Number!

Although this is just a one-year snapshot, what we can deduce from this simple example is that higher-rate taxpayers who use salary sacrifice can boost their pension contributions by 18%.

This means salary sacrifice could have a significant impact on the amount of money you are able to save for retirement.

For example, if you would expect your own pension contributions to eventually grow in value to £100,000 without salary sacrifice, then you can expect them to grow to £118,000 with salary sacrifice.

If you would expect your own pension contributions to grow in value to £200,000 without salary sacrifice, then you can expect them to grow to £236,000 with salary sacrifice ... and so on.

These are significant increases. Remember this extra money is completely **free**! You would not have to save a single penny extra to enjoy this boost to your retirement savings.

The extra money comes about because you and your employer are saving national insurance.

Note, your *total* pension pot will not increase by 18%, just the amount that you were originally contributing personally. Remember Jane's employer was already contributing to her pension before the salary sacrifice took place. Her employer's *original* (pre-salary sacrifice) contributions will not increase under a salary sacrifice arrangement.

How to Calculate Your Own Salary Sacrifice

Let's say you are a higher-rate taxpayer and personally contribute £100 to your pension. The gross contribution is £125 (£100/0.8) and you will receive £25 of higher-rate relief (£125 x 20%). So the actual cost to you is just £75 (£100 - £25).

To get £75 of income in your hands you will have had to earn £129 of salary:

£129 *less* 40% income tax *less* 2% national insurance = £75

So if you sacrifice £129 of salary and stop making pension contributions you will still have the same amount of disposable income to spend.

To perform the same calculation for yourself and calculate how much salary you need to sacrifice just follow these two simple steps:

- **Step 1.** Multiply the amount you personally contribute to your pension by 0.75 – the resulting number is what your pension contributions are actually costing you and takes into account your higher-rate relief.

- **Step 2.** Add back the 40% income tax and 2% national insurance you have paid on this income. To do this divide the result from Step 1 by 0.58:

$$\frac{\text{Step 1}}{0.58}$$

Example
As we know, Jane is a higher-rate taxpayer and personally contributes £2,400 to her pension. The taxman tops this up with £600, so her gross pension contribution is £3,000. Jane's salary sacrifice is calculated as follows:

- ***Step 1.*** *Multiply the amount she personally contributes to her pension by 0.75:*

  £2,400 x 0.75 = £1,800

- ***Step 2.*** *Add back her 40% income tax and 2% national insurance by dividing the result by 0.58:*

  £1,800/0.58 = £3,103

If she sacrifices £3,103 of salary and stops contributing to her pension plan, her disposable income will remain the same.

Her employer will contribute £3,103 to her pension plan, plus an extra £428 (£3,103 x 13.8%). This is the employer's national insurance saving. Her total pension contribution will now be £3,531.

It's important to remember that she can enjoy this free increase to her pension pot **every year.**

Furthermore, this is just her national insurance saving. As a higher-rate taxpayer she will also be enjoying 40% income tax relief on her pension contributions.

A higher-rate taxpayer who personally contributes £2,400 to a pension plan will receive a £600 income tax refund from the taxman so the actual cost is just £1,800. The taxman's top-up will take the total pension contribution to £3,000.

With salary sacrifice the pension contribution then goes up to £3,531 without costing a penny extra.

Chapter 27

How to Convince Your Employer

After over 20 years in the tax publishing business one thing I have learnt is that most tax breaks come with a catch.

With salary sacrifice pensions the catch is you need your employer's co-operation. If your employer isn't already offering a salary sacrifice arrangement, you'll have to get him or her to agree to it and to do the necessary paperwork (see Chapter 29).

How much bargaining power you have with your employer will, of course, depend on how big the company is and how senior you are.

If you are a senior executive at a small or medium-sized company, you should find it relatively easy to get your employer to introduce a salary sacrifice arrangement. If you are a junior employee at a multinational corporation your chances are probably slim.

However, because a salary sacrifice arrangement could increase your pension pot by thousands of pounds, I believe it's worth fighting for tooth and nail.

Fortunately, there are several arguments you can use to convince your employer:

Argument #1 Other Employers Are Doing It

Salary sacrifice pensions are available from some of the country's biggest and most reputable companies, universities and other organisations, including BT, Tesco and the BBC.

To stay competitive in the jobs market your employer should also be offering this benefit.

Argument #2 Easy to Implement

As we will see in Chapter 29, the paperwork is relatively straightforward and may only have to be done once. Having said this, some employers may shy away from introducing a salary sacrifice arrangement if they are currently grappling with their new auto-enrolment duties and if they fear that a salary sacrifice pension arrangement will not be auto-enrolment compliant.

Argument #3 Giving Employees a FREE Pay Increase

This is by far the most powerful argument you can use to convince your employer to introduce a salary sacrifice pension arrangement.

The employee effectively receives a pay increase that doesn't cost the employer anything. The taxman foots the entire bill.

What rational employer would turn down such an opportunity?

Sharing the Savings with Your Employer

If you are struggling to convince your employer to introduce a salary sacrifice pension arrangement, you can offer to share the national insurance savings.

Remember there are two types of national insurance: the type the employee pays and the type the employer pays.

In all the examples so far we have assumed that both the employee's and employer's national insurance savings are paid into the employee's pension plan.

However, to convince your employer to introduce a salary sacrifice pension arrangement you may have to appeal to his selfish side and offer to share the national insurance savings.

Your employer generally pays 13.8% national insurance on every pound you earn over £8,788 (2020/21 figures). It may be necessary to offer your employer, say, half of the employer's national insurance saving (6.9% of the salary sacrifice amount) to co-operate with you.

170

Ideally you should negotiate to have your employer share the national insurance savings for just one year, perhaps to compensate him for time spent doing the necessary paperwork. However, even if your employer insists on a permanent national insurance share, you will still be far better off in most cases with a salary sacrifice pension arrangement.

For example, in Chapter 25 we showed how John, a basic-rate taxpayer, saw his pension contribution go up from £1,250 to £1,673 with a salary sacrifice arrangement – an increase of 34%. This was helped by his employer contributing the full national insurance saving of £203.

If his employer had only agreed to contribute half his saving, John's pension contribution would have increased from £1,250 to £1,571 – an increase of 26%. John is still significantly better off with a salary sacrifice pension.

Similarly, in Chapter 26 we showed how Jane, a higher-rate taxpayer, saw her pension contribution go up from £3,000 to £3,531 with a salary sacrifice arrangement – an increase of 18%. This was helped by her employer contributing the full national insurance saving of £428.

If her employer had only agreed to contribute half the saving Jane's pension contribution would have increased from £3,000 to £3,317 – an increase of 11%. Jane is still better off with a salary sacrifice pension.

Employer Refuses to Share NI Savings

What happens if your employer refuses to share any of the national insurance savings? This is the worst-case scenario but cannot be ruled out.

If you are a basic-rate taxpayer a salary sacrifice pension may still be worth having because your pension contributions will still be approximately 18% higher.

If you are a higher-rate taxpayer, however, a salary sacrifice pension will increase your pension contributions by a paltry 3%. Remember, higher-rate taxpayers only pay 2% national insurance on earnings over £50,000. So a salary sacrifice saves them very little unless some or all of the employer's much larger 13.8% national insurance bill is also added to the pension pot.

In summary, a salary sacrifice arrangement loses most of its attractiveness if you are a higher-rate taxpayer and your employer refuses to share the national insurance savings.

When Your Employer Doesn't Pay NI

Most businesses currently receive an allowance of £4,000 per year to offset against their national insurance bills. Thus in some very small companies – those employing just a few people on low salaries – there may be no employer's national insurance payable.

There's also no employer's national insurance on salary income under the higher-rate threshold (£50,000) paid to under 21s and apprentices under 25.

If the business doesn't have any national insurance to pay, a salary sacrifice will not produce an employer's national insurance saving that can be paid into the employees' pensions.

Summary

- Salary sacrifice requires your employer's approval.

- To convince your employer to introduce salary sacrifice you can use the following arguments:

    - Many big, reputable employers offer salary sacrifice
    - It is relatively easy to implement
    - It allows employers to provide FREE pay increases

- The national insurance savings can be shared with your employer. A basic-rate taxpayer could still end up with a 26% bigger pension pot. A higher-rate taxpayer could still end up with an 11% bigger pension pot.

- If your employer refuses to share any of the national insurance savings, a salary sacrifice arrangement is still worthwhile if you are a basic-rate taxpayer... but not very effective if you are a higher-rate taxpayer.

172

Chapter 28

Salary Sacrifice Drawbacks

With salary sacrifice your gross salary is reduced, so anything that depends on your gross salary could be affected, including your:

- Employment benefits
- Borrowing ability
- Maternity pay

For starters, the general consensus among pension experts is that you should not take part in a salary sacrifice arrangement if your income will fall below the lower earnings limit (currently £6,240).

This is because your entitlement to various state benefits may be affected if your income falls below the lower earnings limit, including state pension, statutory sick pay, maternity pay, incapacity benefit and jobseekers' allowance.

Also, your employer cannot let a salary sacrifice take you under the national minimum wage or national living wage.

Employment Benefits

If a salary sacrifice reduces your gross salary then this could *potentially* also reduce your:

- Future pay increases
- Overtime
- Life insurance cover provided by your employer
- Redundancy payments

Many salary sacrifice arrangements address this issue by making sure all benefits are based on the employee's original salary – often referred to as the reference salary, notional salary or base salary. So if you are currently earning £40,000 and your salary is reduced to £37,000, your employment benefits can be calculated on the basis that you are still earning £40,000.

Borrowing Ability

Any salary reduction could affect your ability to borrow money, for example to buy a house or for any other purpose.

One solution is for your employer to provide the lender with a letter of reference confirming your reference salary. For example, some of the university salary sacrifice documents state that:

"You should quote your current annual salary on mortgage applications and your payslip will substantiate this figure as your annual salary. If The University Payroll Office receives requests for mortgage references from lenders they will quote your current salary i.e. before the reduction."

This potential issue can therefore be addressed. However, there is still a potential risk that some lenders will not accept your reference salary and use the lower post-sacrifice salary.

New State Pension

Since 6 April 2016 the basic state pension and state second pension have been replaced with a flat-rate pension currently worth £175.20 per week – £9,110 per year.

From now on your state pension entitlement is based solely on how many years of national insurance contributions or credits you have – the amount you earn is irrelevant.

Under the previous system your entitlement to the state second pension was based on your earnings and could therefore have been adversely affected by a salary sacrifice.

To qualify for the new state pension you need 35 years of national insurance contributions or credits – five years more than before. If you have less than 35 years you will get a proportion of the full state pension. For example, if you have 28 years of contributions you will get 80%.

To qualify for any state pension you will need a minimum level of contributions, usually 10 years worth. If you have less than this you will not receive any pension.

For those starting their working life after 5 April 2016, the new system is much simpler – you will simply get the flat–rate pension providing you have enough years of national insurance contributions.

If you were working before this date, your eventual state pension will be based on your previous national insurance record (the full value of your previous contributions will be preserved), and your current national insurance record since the switch to the new state pension.

Maternity Pay

A salary sacrifice arrangement could reduce the amount of statutory maternity pay (SMP) to which you are entitled. Statutory maternity pay is based on your contractual earnings which count for national insurance contributions. So if your earnings have been reduced because you sacrificed some salary, the amount of statutory maternity pay you receive may also be reduced.

If a salary sacrifice takes your salary below the lower earnings limit (£6,240 in 2020/21), you will lose your statutory maternity pay entitlement altogether.

How is Statutory Maternity Pay Calculated?

Women are entitled to 52 weeks of maternity leave and 39 weeks of statutory maternity pay.

For the first six weeks you are entitled to receive 90% of your average gross weekly earnings, with no upper limit. So a salary sacrifice could reduce the amount of SMP you receive for the first six weeks.

For the remaining 33 weeks you are entitled to receive the *lesser* of:

- £151.20 per week (2020/21)
- 90% of your average weekly earnings

All except the lowest paid will receive a flat amount of £151.20 per week for this 33-week period, so a salary sacrifice will probably have no effect on this part of your SMP entitlement.

Statutory Maternity Pay – Effect on the Employer

Employers are liable to pay statutory maternity pay but can get most of it refunded.

If the employer's total payments of class 1 national insurance are £45,000 or less the employer can recover 103% of the SMP paid.

The extra amount is to compensate for the employer's national insurance payable on the SMP.

If the employer's total class 1 national insurance payments are more than £45,000 per year, the employer can recover 92% of the SMP paid.

Employer vs Employee

With salary sacrifice pensions the idea is that neither the employee nor the employer ends up worse off. However, salary sacrifice pension arrangements could prove costly for employers when their staff are on parental leave.

The general rule is that employer pension contributions must continue to be made as normal while an employee is on paid parental leave. With salary sacrifice the employer's pension contributions are larger than normal so the cost could be higher.

Maternity Allowance

Maternity allowance is paid to women who are employed but not entitled to SMP. Maternity allowance is based on your earnings, so a salary sacrifice arrangement may reduce your entitlement to maternity allowance.

Chapter 29

How to Implement a Salary Sacrifice Pension

It is important to point out that salary sacrifice must be a *contractual agreement*, not an informal arrangement between you and your employer.

In other words, you have to change your employment contract and this should to be done in writing.

It may be possible to change your contract of employment by using a simple agreement letter, signed by both you and your employer. Many pension companies provide sample documents. This letter should be kept with your employment contract.

The new agreement must state what benefit is being received in exchange for the sacrificed salary.

It's important that the potential future salary is given up before it is treated as received for tax and national insurance purposes. Your terms of employment must be changed *before* the salary sacrifice commences.

HMRC is not against salary sacrifice but could challenge the arrangement if it has not been set up correctly and the paperwork is not in order.

Salary Sacrifice and Auto Enrolment

The operation of a salary sacrifice arrangement is separate from the automatic enrolment provisions (see Chapter 21), although the Pension Regulator states that employers can run the two in parallel when complying with their employer duties.

An employer can ask an employee who must be automatically enrolled whether they want to use a salary sacrifice arrangement. However, active membership of a pension scheme cannot depend on the employee agreeing to use salary sacrifice. If the employee does not agree to salary sacrifice, the employer must automatically enrol them into the pension scheme with an alternative method of making pension contributions.

The qualifying earnings used to work out the minimum pension contribution required under auto-enrolment are based on the post-sacrifice level of salary.

However, some commentators argue that it is better to base contributions on the pre-sacrificed salary to maintain good relations with employees.

Getting HMRC Approval

HM Revenue & Customs does not have to be notified of salary sacrifice arrangements. However, after the arrangement is set up employers can ask HMRC to advise on the tax and national insurance consequences.

This gives the employer reassurance the arrangement has been implemented correctly.

HMRC will probably want to see evidence that the employment contracts have been changed correctly and payslips, before and after the sacrifice.

For more information:

www.gov.uk/guidance/non-statutory-clearance-service-guidance

Payslips and P60s

Strictly speaking, your new post-salary-sacrifice payslip should not show your old salary, with the sacrificed amount shown as a deduction.

However, HMRC's guidance notes state that if the employment contract has been changed correctly, the payslip is less important.

However, if there are issues surrounding the employment contract, the payslip may be used to determine whether the salary sacrifice is valid.

HMRC recognises that some payroll software can only store one value for the employee's salary. This could create problems when calculating overtime and other benefits based on the higher pre-sacrifice reference salary.

However, as long as the contract has been modified correctly, and makes it clear that the employee is entitled to a reduced salary and specified benefits, HMRC should not invalidate the salary sacrifice.

HMRC's guidance notes point out that non-taxable benefits-in-kind must not be carried forward to the P60.

Finally, I would strongly recommend speaking to an advisor who has experience of salary sacrifice pensions and auto-enrolment before diving in and setting one up yourself.

Part 7

Company Directors

Chapter 30

Introduction

Company directors, just like regular employees, can contribute up to 100% of their 'relevant UK earnings' to a pension but typically not more than £40,000 (the annual allowance).

Your relevant UK earnings will include your:

- Salary and any bonus
- Taxable benefits in kind

For example, a company director with a salary of £20,000 can make a cash contribution of up to £16,000. The taxman will top this up with £4,000 of basic-rate tax relief for a gross pension contribution of £20,000.

A company director with a salary of £50,000 can make a cash contribution of up to £32,000. The taxman will top this up with £8,000 of basic-rate tax relief for a gross pension contribution of £40,000. He can make an additional pension contribution of £10,000 gross if he has unused annual allowance from any of the previous three tax years.

(Of course, as we saw in Chapter 4, the director may not want to make such a large contribution in practice because he would not receive higher-rate tax relief on the whole contribution.)

Company Pension Contributions

As a company owner you can also get your company (your employer) to make pension contributions on your behalf. Company pension contributions are always paid *gross* (there is no top up from the taxman) but the company will normally enjoy corporation tax relief on the payment.

For example, a company paying 19% corporation tax and making a pension contribution of £10,000 can claim corporation tax relief of £1,900 (£10,000 x 19%).

Pension contributions made by employers are not restricted by the level of the employee's earnings. A company pension contribution can be bigger than the director's earnings. However, there are other restrictions on company pension contributions:

Firstly, total pension contributions by you and your company must not exceed the £40,000 annual allowance, although any unused allowance from the previous three tax years can be carried forward and used to cover contributions made by both you and the company. (High income earners may be subject to a lower annual allowance – see Chapter 20.)

Secondly, the company may be denied corporation tax relief on any pension contributions made on behalf of directors, if the taxman views them as 'excessive'. We'll return to this point later.

In this part of the guide we explain why pension contributions are an attractive alternative to dividends.

We also answer the important question asked by many company owners: "Who should make the pension contributions: me or the company?"

However, before doing that it's important to explain how company owners often structure their pay to reduce income tax.

Chapter 31

Salary or Dividend?

Most small company owners are both directors and shareholders. This means they can withdraw both salaries and dividends from their companies. Salaries are subject to income tax and national insurance, dividends are subject to income tax only.

Taking a big salary is usually very expensive because of the national insurance cost. Up to 12% national insurance will have to be paid by the company owner personally and an extra 13.8% will usually have to be paid by the company.

But taking all the profits out as dividends is not the best solution either for most small company owners because this means subjecting all the company's profits to corporation tax (dividends are paid out of after-tax profits).

The optimal solution in many cases is to pay a small salary that is tax deductible in the company's hands and mostly free from national insurance in the hands of the company owner.

What is the Optimal Salary for 2020/21?

There are three important income tax and national insurance thresholds for the current 2020/21 tax year:

- Employer's national insurance   £8,788
- Employee's national insurance   £9,500
- Income tax   £12,500

For many company owners taking a salary equal to one of these thresholds is optimal.

In the chapters that follow we will assume that the company owner takes a salary of £9,500. A salary of £9,500 will not attract any employee's national insurance and, providing the company owner has no other income, will also be free from income tax. A small amount of *employer's* national insurance will be payable, compared with a completely tax-free salary of £8,788, but the corporation tax relief on the extra payment generally outweighs the national insurance cost.

A salary of £9,500 will not be optimal for everyone. Where the company owner has taxable income from other sources, a small tax saving of around £50 can be achieved by taking a salary of £8,788 instead of £9,500.

If your company does not use up its £4,000 national insurance employment allowance paying salaries to other employees, there may be spare employment allowance for the directors own salaries. In these circumstances a salary of up to £12,500 is generally more tax efficient. In some cases (when the company owner has significant income from other sources), sticking with a salary of £9,500 may be better from a tax saving standpoint.

Note that the employment allowance is not available to companies where a single director is the sole employee. According to HMRC guidance, the employment allowance also cannot be claimed if there are other employees BUT the director's salary is the only one on which employer's national insurance is payable. Many tax experts disagree with this interpretation of the rules.

There are many other tax and non-tax factors that may influence your salary decision. Some company owners may wish to pay themselves a bigger salary because, although strictly speaking not "optimal", this lets them take a bigger chunk of income out of the company on a regular basis, without some of the hassle that comes with paying dividends (for example, making sure the company has sufficient distributable profits and that dividends are properly declared).

For a complete discussion of this topic see the Taxcafe guide *Salary versus Dividends*.

Once they've paid themselves a small salary, many company owners take the rest of their income as dividends.

How Dividends Are Taxed

Dividends are subject to income tax but not national insurance. Also, the income tax rates on dividends are lower than the income tax rates on salaries because dividends are paid out of a company's *after-tax* profits: the money has already been taxed in the company's hands, whereas salaries are a tax deductible expense.

The tax treatment of dividends was completely changed with effect from 6 April 2016.

Dividend tax credits have been abolished, so it is no longer necessary to gross up your cash dividends to calculate your tax. All tax calculations now work with cash dividends only and are therefore a lot simpler.

(I generally refer to the amount of dividend actually paid, or deemed to be paid, as the "cash" dividend. This does not necessarily mean that it is literally paid in cash, as dividends are sometimes paid by way of accounting entries.)

While simpler tax calculations are the good news, the bad news is that the current tax rates for cash dividends are 7.5% higher than the previous ones.

The first £2,000 of dividend income you receive is, however, tax free thanks to the "dividend nil rate band", also known as the "dividend allowance". The dividend allowance was cut from £5,000 to £2,000 on 6th April 2018.

For those receiving dividends in excess of the dividend allowance, the following income tax rates apply (the old effective rates are included for comparison):

	Old	Current
Basic-rate taxpayers	0%	7.5%
Higher-rate taxpayers	25%	32.5%
Additional-rate taxpayers	30.6%	38.1%

Overall Tax Rates on Dividend Income

Because income paid as dividends is taxed twice (first in the hands of the company and second in the hands of the shareholder) it's easy to lose sight of how much tax is being paid overall.

As a company owner you are likely to be equally concerned about your company's tax bill as your own, so it's worth showing the overall combined tax rate on dividend income. With companies currently paying 19% corporation tax, the total tax rates on dividend income are as follows:

	Total Tax Rate (rounded)
Basic-rate taxpayers	25%
Higher-rate taxpayers	45%
Additional-rate taxpayers	50%

A company with £100 of profit will pay £19 corporation tax, leaving £81 to pay as dividends. Ignoring the £2,000 dividend allowance, a higher-rate taxpayer will pay £26 tax on this income (£81 x 32.5%), so the total tax on the £100 profit is £45, i.e. 45%.

The above tax rates are significantly higher than the regular income tax rates that apply to most types of income (20% for basic-rate taxpayers, 40% for higher-rate taxpayers and 45% for additional-rate taxpayers).

This is because the Government wanted to level the playing field between company owners (who often don't pay any national insurance) and self-employed business owners and regular employees, who pay national insurance on most of their earnings.

From a tax planning perspective, once they've used up the £2,000 dividend allowance, company owners may now be better off paying themselves certain types of income that are taxed at "regular" income tax rates in preference to dividends, wherever possible. An obvious example would be rental income (but not salary income if national insurance is also payable).

Finally, please note that I am not recommending that you structure your pay in the way described in this chapter. You should always speak to an accountant about your own optimal pay structure.

Chapter 32

Pension Contributions: Better than Dividends?

Following the increase in dividend tax rates, some company owners are probably paying themselves smaller dividends and getting their companies to make pension contributions instead.

There are several reasons why pension contributions are attractive:

- Like salaries, company pension contributions enjoy corporation tax relief. In other words, they're a tax deductible business expense.

- When you eventually withdraw money from your pension, 25% can be taken tax free.

- There is no national insurance on pension income.

- Pension income is taxed at the "regular" income tax rates, typically 20% or 40%. By contrast, the combined tax rate (corporation tax and income tax) on dividend income is currently 25% for basic-rate taxpayers and 45% for higher-rate taxpayers.

- When you start withdrawing money from your pension, you could find yourself in a lower tax bracket than you are now (most retirees are basic-rate taxpayers).

Putting all this together, there's a strong possibility that you will pay tax on your pension income at an effective rate of just 15% (and possibly lower), compared with the 25% or 45% you are currently paying on your dividend income.

There is, of course, a major drawback with pensions: your money is locked away until you are 55 (probably rising to 57 in 2028). Nevertheless, when you do reach the minimum retirement age, you can now make unlimited withdrawals.

Example – Higher-rate Taxpayer

Lesleyanne is a company owner and a higher-rate taxpayer.

Let's say she is trying to choose between taking an additional £100 of the company's profit as a dividend or getting the company to invest £100 in her self-invested personal pension (SIPP).

With a dividend the company will pay 19% corporation tax, leaving £81 to distribute. After paying income tax at 32.5% Lesleyanne will be left with around £55. The total tax rate will be roughly 45%.

A company pension contribution will enjoy corporation tax relief so the whole £100 will go straight into Lesleyanne's SIPP. Ignoring investment growth (it doesn't affect the outcome), when she eventually withdraws the money from her pension the first £25 will be tax free and the remaining £75 will subject to income tax.

If Lesleyanne is a basic-rate taxpayer when she retires she will pay 20% tax (£15), leaving her with £85. Thus her effective tax rate will be 15%.

If Lesleyanne is a higher-rate taxpayer when she retires (for example, if she ends up with a significant amount of other assets such as buy-to-let properties) she will effectively pay 40% tax on her taxable pension income (£30), leaving her with £70 overall. Thus her effective tax rate will be 30%, which is still better than the 45% currently payable on her dividend income.

It's also possible that some of Lesleyanne's pension withdrawals will be tax free thanks to her income tax personal allowance. In that case her effective tax rate will be 0%!

This example shows that, for company owners who have not already built up significant pension savings, a company pension contribution is an extremely attractive alternative to additional dividend income.

Of course, one must never lose sight of the fact that your pension savings are placed in a locked box until you are at least 55. So a company pension contribution is only an attractive alternative to a dividend if you have already withdrawn enough money from your company to cover your living costs.

In the previous example the company owner got her company to make a pension contribution to avoid the 32.5% tax payable on dividend income. But are company pension contributions worth making if you're a basic-rate taxpayer? Let's find out:

Example – Basic-rate Taxpayer

Poppy is a company owner and a basic-rate taxpayer.

She too is trying to choose between taking £100 of the company's profit as a dividend and a £100 company pension contribution.

With a dividend the company will pay 19% corporation tax, leaving £81 to distribute as a dividend. After paying income tax at 7.5% Poppy will be left with around £75. The total tax rate will be roughly 25%.

With a company pension contribution the whole £100 will go straight into Poppy's SIPP. Ignoring investment growth, when Poppy eventually withdraws the money from her pension the first £25 will be tax free and the remaining £75 will subject to income tax.

Like Lesleyanne, the effective tax rate on her pension income will be:

- *0% if covered by her personal allowance*
- *15% if she is a basic-rate taxpayer*
- *30% if she is a higher-rate taxpayer*

Once again, if Poppy has enough income to cover her living costs, a company pension contribution is an attractive alternative to additional dividend income... unless Poppy ends up wealthier in retirement and becomes a higher-rate taxpayer.

This could happen if, for example, she eventually inherits a significant amount of money and the investment income takes her over the higher-rate threshold.

If she expects to become a higher-rate taxpayer in the future she may be better off taking as much dividend income as she can taxed at just 7.5%, while she can, and investing the surplus funds in an ISA.

Auto-Enrolment

In recent years the Government has rolled out a system of compulsory pensions called auto-enrolment. Essentially it's an extra tax on employers.

Only employees earning more than £10,000 and aged from 22 to state pension age need to be *automatically* enrolled into a pension. Some older and younger employees and those who earn less than £10,000 also have certain workplace pension rights.

According to the Pension Regulator a company does not have any automatic-enrolment duties when:

- It has just one director, with no other staff

- It has a number of directors, none of whom has an employment contract, with no other staff

- It has a number of directors, only one of whom has an employment contract, with no other staff

A contract of employment does not have to be in writing. However, according to the Pension Regulator, if there is no written contract of employment, or other evidence of an intention to create an employer/worker relationship between the company and the director, it will not argue that an employment contract exists.

If a director does not have an employment contract they are always exempt from automatic enrolment. If a director has a contract of employment and there are other people working for the company with an employment contract, they are not exempt.

Depending on their age and earnings, they may qualify for automatic enrolment but the company can decide whether to automatically enrol them into a pension. However, the director has the right to join a pension scheme at any time and the company cannot refuse to enrol them (although in practice this problem will not arise in most owner-managed companies).

If the company decides not to enrol any employed director who is eligible for automatic enrolment, and it has no other eligible staff, it does not need to set up a pension scheme. However, it will need to make a 'declaration of compliance'.

Chapter 33

Pension Contributions: You or the Company?

In the previous chapter we showed that company pension contributions can be an attractive alternative to dividends.

However, company directors can also make pension contributions *personally*, so a key question is:

> *"Who should make the contributions: the director or the company?"*

Before the increase in dividend tax rates it was often more tax efficient for a small pension contribution to be made by the company director personally.

At present it is often tax efficient in most cases to get your company to make the pension contributions.

Company Owner Pension Contributions

As we know from previous chapters, when you make pension contributions *personally* (as opposed to getting your company to make them) the taxman will top up your savings by paying cash directly into your pension. Effectively for every £80 you invest, the taxman will put in an extra £20.

Why £20? Your contributions are treated as having been paid out of income that has already been taxed at the 20% basic rate of income tax.

The company that manages your pension plan – usually an insurance company or SIPP provider – will claim this money for you from the taxman and credit it to your account.

So whatever contribution you make personally, divide it by 0.80 and you'll get the total amount that is invested in your pension pot (your gross pension contribution).

Example

Peter is a company owner who takes most of his income as dividends. He invests £800 in a self-invested personal pension (SIPP). The taxman will top up his pension with £200 of basic-rate tax relief which means he'll have £1,000 in his pension pot:

$$£800/0.80 = £1,000$$

If Peter is a higher-rate taxpayer he can also claim higher-rate tax relief when he completes his tax return. This is given by increasing his basic-rate band by the amount of his gross pension contribution.

Example continued

Peter's gross pension contribution is £1,000 so his basic-rate band will be increased by £1,000. This means £1,000 of his dividend income will be taxed at 7.5% instead of 32.5%, i.e. a 25% saving. Thus, Peter's higher-rate tax relief is:

$$£1,000 \times 25\% = £250$$

In total Peter will enjoy £450 of tax relief (£200 basic-rate relief plus £250 higher-rate tax relief). Peter's total tax relief is 45% of his £1,000 gross pension contribution.

Company Directors with Small Salaries

To obtain tax relief on your pension contributions they have to stay within certain limits:

- **Earnings**. Contributions made by you *personally* must not exceed your 'relevant UK earnings'. Earnings include your salary, bonus and taxable benefits in kind but do NOT include your dividends.

- **The £40,000 Annual Allowance.** Total pension contributions by you and your company must not exceed £40,000 per year, although it is possible to carry forward any unused annual allowance from the three previous tax years. The annual allowance is reduced if your "adjusted income" exceeds £240,000 (see Chapter 20).

For a company director taking the 'optimal' tax-free salary of £9,500, the maximum pension contribution that can be made in 2020/21 is therefore £9,500.

This is the maximum *gross* contribution. The director would personally invest £7,600 (£9,500 x 80%) and the taxman will top this up with £1,900 of basic-rate tax relief for a total gross contribution of £9,500.

For a company director taking a salary of £12,500, the maximum gross pension contribution is £12,500. The director would personally invest £10,000 (£12,500 x 80%) and the taxman will top this up with £2,500 of basic-rate tax relief for a total gross contribution of £12,500.

Directors who want to make bigger pension contributions personally have to pay themselves bigger salaries. However, this is usually not an attractive option because a bigger salary may be subject to both employee's and employer's national insurance (at 12% and 13.8% respectively).

Company Pension Contributions

As a company owner you can also get your company (your employer) to make pension contributions on your behalf. Company pension contributions are always paid *gross* (there is no top up from the taxman) but the company will normally enjoy corporation tax relief on the payment. For example, a company paying 19% corporation tax can make a pension contribution of £10,000 and enjoy £1,900 tax relief.

Note, you do not need a dedicated company pension scheme to make company pension contributions. Most firms that offer SIPPs have special forms that allow your company to pay directly into your pension (although these plans may not be qualifying schemes for auto-enrolment purposes).

How much can your company contribute? Unlike the contributions that you make personally, the company's contributions are NOT restricted by the size of your salary.

In other words, the company can make a pension contribution that is bigger than your salary.

However, there are other restrictions on company contributions:

- Total pension contributions by you and your company must not exceed the annual allowance (typically £40,000), although you can carry forward any unused allowance from the previous three tax years.

- The company may be denied corporation tax relief on any pension contributions made on behalf of directors, if the taxman views them as 'excessive' (see below).

Corporation Tax Relief on Pension Contributions

Unlike the pension contributions that you make personally, tax relief for company pension contributions is not automatic.

Company contributions will only be a tax deductible expense for corporation tax purposes if they are incurred wholly and exclusively for the purposes of the trade.

There is a danger that HMRC will deny corporation tax relief for 'excessive' pension contributions. In practice this is relatively rare.

When determining whether company pension contributions qualify for corporation tax relief, HMRC will look at the total remuneration package of the director. The total package (including salary, pension contributions and other benefits in kind) must not be excessive relative to the work the individual carries out and his or her responsibilities.

Relevant factors may include:

- The number of hours you work, your experience and your level of responsibility in the company.

- The pay of unconnected employees in your company and other companies who perform duties of similar value.

- The pay required to recruit someone to take over your duties.

- The company's financial performance.

Extra care may be necessary in the event of a large one-off company pension contribution.

It may be sensible to document the commercial justification (e.g. strong recent financial performance of the company) in the minutes of a directors' board meeting and hold a shareholders' meeting to approve the contribution.

In some cases, when a much larger than normal contribution is made, it may be necessary to spread tax relief over a number of years. These spreading rules will not affect most small companies and only kick in when the excess contributions amount to £500,000 or more.

Although the risk that your company will be denied corporation tax relief may be small, it is important to stress that, when it comes to company pension contributions, unlike contributions made by individuals, there is no cast-iron guarantee that the company will enjoy tax relief.

That's why I would recommend speaking to a tax advisor before your company starts making significant contributions.

Pension Contributions – You or the Company?

Using a couple of case studies we will now compare company pension contributions with pension contributions made personally by company owners to see which is most tax efficient.

Case Study 1 – Basic-rate Taxpayer

Eva owns Cassidy Ltd. She is a basic-rate taxpayer and pays herself a small tax-free salary of £9,500 and takes the rest of her income as dividends.

In 2020/21 she decides to make a £1,000 pension contribution. If Cassidy Ltd makes the contribution it can pay £1,000 directly into Eva's SIPP.

If instead Eva pays herself a dividend to fund a pension contribution that she makes personally, the company will pay 19% corporation tax leaving Eva with £810.

Eva holds onto £10 and invests £800 in her SIPP. The taxman will add £200 of basic-rate tax relief, leaving her with the same amount in her pension – £1,000.

But that's not the end of the matter: Eva will still have to pay 7.5% tax on her £810 dividend – roughly £60.

Eva is worse off by £50: £60 less the £10 of saved dividend income.

Thus, if you're a basic-rate taxpayer, for every £1,000 that ends up in your pension you will have to pay an additional 5% in tax.

In this case a company pension contribution is clearly more tax efficient than a contribution made personally by the director.

Other Important Points

If Eva wants more than £9,500 invested in her pension, making the contribution personally will be even more expensive.

She would have to pay herself a bigger salary and this could result in a significant amount of national insurance becoming payable. This is because any pension contribution you make personally cannot exceed your earnings (i.e. salary).

The additional salary would attract 12% employee's national insurance and 13.8% employer's national insurance (unless there is spare employment allowance).

Case Study 2 – Higher-rate Taxpayer

This time we'll assume Eva is a *higher-rate taxpayer* and again wants to make a £1,000 pension contribution.

If Cassidy Ltd makes the contribution it can pay £1,000 directly into Eva's SIPP. Alternatively Eva can pay herself an £810 dividend, hold onto £10 and invest £800 in her SIPP. The taxman will add £200 of basic-rate tax relief, resulting in the same gross pension contribution of £1,000.

Again, that's not the end of the matter. Eva still has to pay income tax on the additional dividend.

With a gross pension contribution of £1,000, Eva's basic-rate band will be increased by £1,000. This means the £810 dividend will be taxed at just 7.5%, not 32.5%, so the tax is roughly £60.

Furthermore, an additional £190 of her other dividend income will also be taxed at 7.5% instead of 32.5%, saving her an extra £48.

All in all a £1,000 pension contribution made by the director is only £2 more expensive than a contribution made by the company:

£60 income tax - £48 higher-rate relief - £10 saved dividend = £2

In this case a company pension contribution is again more tax efficient than a contribution made personally by the director but the difference is tiny.

Because the saving is so small it will probably be other factors that determine whether the company or the individual makes the pension contributions.

Other Important Points

Note that if Eva wants to enjoy full higher-rate tax relief on a gross pension contribution of £9,500 (i.e. equal to her salary), she must have at least £9,500 of dividend income above the higher-rate threshold (income of at least £59,500 in 2020/21).

If Eva wants to make a pension contribution bigger than £9,500 personally she will have to pay herself a bigger salary and this may result in a significant amount of national insurance becoming payable.

Lifetime ISA versus Company Pension Contribution

In Chapter 15 we examined the new Lifetime ISA. Like pensions they attract a top up from the Government but, unlike pensions, ALL the money you take out will be tax free.

Let's say a company owner who is a basic-rate taxpayer is trying to decide between a £1,000 company pension contribution and using a dividend to fund a Lifetime ISA contribution.

A £1,000 pension contribution will attract corporation tax relief so the whole £1,000 will go directly into the company owner's pension.

If the same money is used to fund a dividend, the company will pay 19% corporation tax leaving £810 to pay out. After paying 7.5% income tax the company owner will be left with around £750 to invest in a Lifetime ISA. Adding the Government bonus the company owner will end up with £938 in his Lifetime ISA.

However, when the company owner retires all withdrawals from the Lifetime ISA will be tax free, whereas only 25% of the money withdrawn from the pension will be tax free. The rest will be taxed at 20% if he is a basic-rate taxpayer.

If we ignore investment growth to keep the example simple (it doesn't affect the outcome), with a Lifetime ISA the company owner will end up with £938, with a pension he will end up with just £850 after tax.

Thus, if you're a basic-rate taxpayer, your retirement income could be 10.3% higher with a <u>Lifetime ISA</u>

What about higher-rate taxpayers? Once again a £1,000 pension contribution will attract corporation tax relief so the whole £1,000 will go directly into the company owner's pension.

If the same money is used to fund a dividend, the company will pay 19% corporation tax leaving £810 to pay out. After paying 32.5% income tax the company owner will be left with £547 to invest in his Lifetime ISA. Adding the Government bonus the company owner will end up with £684 in his Lifetime ISA.

When the company owner retires all withdrawals from the Lifetime ISA will be tax free, whereas only 25% of the money withdrawn from the pension will be tax free. The rest will be taxed at 20% if he is now a basic-rate taxpayer (most retirees end up as basic-rate taxpayers).

Ignoring investment growth again, with a Lifetime ISA the company owner will end up with £684, with a pension he will end up with £850 after tax.

Thus, your retirement income could be 24% higher with a _pension_.

However, if the company owner is a higher-rate taxpayer when he retires (e.g. if he has a lot of income from other sources, e.g. rental property) he will end up with £700 from a pension, compared with £684 from a Lifetime ISA. The difference is small and the investment decision will probably be based on other factors.

Summary

- Company pension contributions are currently more tax efficient than contributions made personally by directors.

- The additional saving is very small if the director is a higher-rate taxpayer.

- If you want to make a pension contribution bigger than your existing company salary it is usually more tax efficient to get the company to make the contribution, rather than pay yourself a bigger salary which may have a significant national insurance cost.

- Tax relief for company pension contributions is not automatic – tax relief could be denied if the contributions are viewed as excessive, although this is rare in practice.

- A Lifetime ISA is an attractive alternative to a company pension contribution if you are a basic-rate taxpayer, although you can only invest £4,000 per year and must be under 40 to open one. Pension contributions may be a more attractive alternative if you are a higher-rate taxpayer.

Chapter 34

Taking a Loan from Your Small Self-Administered Scheme (SSAS)

In Chapter 37 we will see how your pension savings can be used to buy commercial property.

This isn't the only way your pension savings can be used to help your business.

Your pension pot can also be used to make a loan to your company.

To do this you will probably have to set up a "small self-administered scheme" (SSAS).

A SSAS is a type of occupational pension scheme, typically established by the owner-managers of a small company (the "sponsoring employer").

SSAS Basics

Although a self-invested personal pension (SIPP) can be used to buy commercial property, a SIPP cannot be used to make a loan to your company.

All pension schemes can make loans to *third parties* but loans to members (or those connected to members) are generally not allowed.

Loans to the sponsoring employers of occupational pension schemes are one exception, however. A SSAS is an occupational scheme and can therefore lend money to the company that sets it up.

A loan cannot be made to the individual members of the pension scheme or their close relatives or other companies controlled by the members (unless those companies are sponsoring employers of the pension scheme too).

A pension loan can be used for a variety of reasons, for example to buy equipment or stock for the business. However, it cannot be used to a keep a failing company afloat or to directly benefit the members.

A SSAS will typically have no more than 11 members and each member will be a "member trustee" with power over how the money is invested. This exempts the SSAS from certain aspects of the pensions legislation, giving it more flexibility.

Small self-administered schemes are offered by a number of specialist pension companies. They provide all the documentation to establish the SSAS, register it with HMRC, act as the "professional trustee" and manage the day-to-day administration.

Setting up and running a SSAS is more expensive than a conventional SIPP so there's no point using one unless you need the extra flexibility.

For example, one well-known pension company I looked at charges £1,250 to set up a SSAS plus a minimum annual fee of £960. A fee of at least £980 is levied to arrange a loan from the pension scheme, plus at least £240 per year to monitor the loan repayments.

There are also quite a few additional one-off and ongoing charges, including setting up the pension scheme's bank account and handling various aspects of its administration. Some of these fees are fixed, others are levied on a time cost basis (something which always makes me nervous).

Further fees may also be incurred when taking out a loan from the pension scheme, for example obtaining a professional valuation for the assets used as security.

Costs vary from pension company to pension company. You can find out what's on offer by simply doing internet searches using phrases that include "SSAS".

Fees can be paid by the sponsoring company rather than the pension scheme.

Pension Loans – The Rules

Borrowing money from your pension may be a lot more attractive than borrowing from a bank or other conventional lender.

However, it's important to note that your pension scheme cannot give your company a soft loan with no interest payable and flexible repayment terms.

There are several rules that have to be obeyed to avoid so-called "unauthorised payment" tax charges:

Interest Rate

The minimum interest rate that must be charged is set out in HMRC's Prescribed Interest Rates for Authorised Employer Loans.

The interest rate must be *at least* 1% higher than the average of the base lending rates of six big UK banks: Bank of Scotland, Barclays, HSBC, Lloyds, Natwest and RBS.

The average rate is rounded up to the nearest 0.25%.

The current minimum interest rate that must be used can be found on HMRC's website under "Interest charged on underpaid quarterly instalment payments":

https://tinyurl.com/emploanrates

The current minimum interest rate is 1.10%.

Higher interest rates can be charged and some of the case studies on the pension companies' websites use interest rates closer to 10%.

The point is that, even if a high rate of interest is charged, at least "it's all kept in the family": the interest payments go from *your* company to *your* pension scheme.

The interest payments will be a tax deductible business expense for the company and tax-free income for the pension scheme (because pension schemes don't pay tax on their investment income).

Security

The loan has to be secured by means of a first charge over assets with a value equal to the loan plus all the interest payable on the loan.

The company may be prevented from taking a pension loan if it already has a "floating charge" over its assets.

Some pension administrators insist that the security must be in the form of land or bricks and mortar property.

Other pension companies accept security in the form of intellectual property owned by the company (for example its trademark, customer database etc).

The asset does not have to be owned by the company.

Whatever asset is used it will have to be independently valued, which will result in additional professional fees being incurred.

Using residential property as security is heavily frowned upon because pension schemes are prohibited from owning residential property in most circumstances.

If the company were to default on the loan, enforcement by the pension scheme of its charge over the property will result in it acquiring a further interest in the taxable property, which will result in unauthorised payment tax charges.

Many pension companies will not allow residential property to be used as security.

Maximum Loan

The loan must not exceed 50% of the net asset value of the pension scheme. So you cannot lend all your pension savings to your company.

Any excess above 50% is treated as an unauthorised payment.

This calculation is performed when the loan is taken out. It doesn't matter if the pension scheme's assets fall in value thereafter.

Length of Loan

The maximum term of the loan is five years. The loan can be rolled over once for another five years in certain circumstances if the company is in genuine financial difficulty.

Repaying the Loan

The loan must be repaid in equal instalments of capital and interest, with at least one payment per year.

If payments fall short an unauthorised payment is deemed to have been made by the pension scheme.

The trustees must take any action necessary to ensure that the loan is repaid, even if this means forcing the company into liquidation.

Unauthorised Payments

If the above rules are broken this could result in an unauthorised payment from the pension scheme.

Unauthorised payments are subject to prohibitive tax charges:

- Unauthorised payment charge – 40% payable by the company

- Scheme sanction charge – 15% payable by the pension scheme administrator (40% if the unauthorised payment charge has not been paid)

- Unauthorised payment surcharge – 15% payable by the company if the unauthorised payments exceed 25% of the value of the pension scheme.

Are Pension Loans a Good Idea?

So is it a good idea to get your company to borrow money from your pension?

One danger is you could end up putting most of your eggs into one basket. If your business goes belly up, you could end up losing a big chunk of your retirement savings as well.

For the same reason it could be argued that business owners should never borrow against their homes.

These three major assets – your business, your pension and your home – should, where possible, be kept completely separate.

This may be a bit unrealistic in practice, however. Borrowing money from a bank is often just as risky for the company owners themselves because banks will usually insist on personal guarantees, typically putting the family home at risk.

In any case why shouldn't an experienced business owner tap their pension pot for a loan if the money will be invested prudently in their business?

Although borrowing from your pension may be acceptable in certain circumstances, I think it would be bordering on insanity to transfer out of a final salary scheme for this purpose.

Are Pension Loans Tax Efficient?

Earlier it was mentioned that, if your company borrows money from your pension scheme, the interest payments will be a tax deductible business expense for the company and tax-free income for the pension scheme.

Does this mean that borrowing money from your pension is tax efficient? Not really. If your company borrowed money from a bank the interest payments would also be tax deductible expense. And the money left in your pension scheme could be invested somewhere else and the investment returns would also be tax free.

However, borrowing from your pension could be less costly overall.

Example – Borrowing from Pension

Jacinda's company, Kiwi Holidays Ltd, needs £100,000 to buy some new equipment.

Jacinda has £200,000 of pension savings, recently transferred into a SSAS.

Let's say Kiwi Holidays borrows £100,000 from the pension scheme and pays 5% interest. For simplicity's sake we will assume the loan is for just one year. The company uses its sales income to repay the loan.

One year later, after the loan is repaid, Jacinda's pension pot will have an additional £5,000 of tax-free interest.

Jacinda's company will have paid out £5,000 interest, with corporation tax relief available on the full amount.

The company will also have paid out £100,000 repaying the initial loan amount but will have £100,000 more equipment. It will probably be able to claim full corporation tax relief on the £100,000 of spending thanks to the annual investment allowance.

Example – Borrowing from a Bank

The facts are exactly the same except this time Jacinda's company borrows from a bank instead of her pension.

Let's say Kiwi Holidays pays 5% interest on the bank loan and her pension savings earn 5% interest when invested elsewhere.

One year later Jacinda's pension pot will have an additional £5,000 of tax-free interest, just as in the above example.

Jacinda's company will have paid out £5,000 interest, with corporation tax relief available on the full amount, just as in the above example.

And just as in the above example, the company will have paid out £100,000 repaying the initial loan amount but will have £100,000 more equipment.

In summary, from a *tax* perspective, borrowing from your pension is exactly the same as borrowing from a bank.

However, Jacinda may end up better off overall if the bank charges her company more interest than she can earn on her pension investments.

Example Revised – Borrowing from Bank

Let's say Kiwi Holidays pays 10% interest on the bank loan and her pension savings earn just 5% interest when invested elsewhere.

One year later Jacinda's pension pot will have an additional £5,000 of tax-free interest, just as in the above examples.

But Jacinda's company will have paid out £10,000 interest to the bank. Tax relief can, of course, be claimed on this interest, just as in the previous examples.

The company will also pay out £100,000 repaying the initial loan amount but will have £100,000 more equipment, just as in the above examples.

Jacinda's company ends up with £5,000 less cash by borrowing from a bank (although almost £1,000 of this will be recovered in additional corporation tax relief).

So it would appear that company owners are better off borrowing from their pensions if the interest rate charged by a third party lender is higher than the return that can be earned on the pension scheme's investments.

When comparing bank borrowing with pension scheme borrowing it's important to take account of all the costs. As we saw earlier, setting up and running a SSAS, and making arrangements to take a loan, will result in a variety of fees and charges.

Borrowing from the Company Owners

A company can also borrow money from the *company owners* themselves.

The company owners can charge the company interest and, as in all the above examples, the company will be able to claim corporation tax relief on the interest payments, as long as the interest rate charged is not unreasonable.

The company owner is not obliged to charge the company interest, although this is often advisable.

The interest payments from the company will be taxable income in the hands of the company owner. However, it's possible to receive up to £6,000 of tax-free interest income every year thanks to the personal savings allowance and starting rate band.

The personal savings allowance allows you to earn up to £1,000 of tax-free interest if you are a basic-rate taxpayer and £500 if you are a higher-rate taxpayer (nothing if you are an additional-rate taxpayer).

The starting rate band allows you to earn up to £5,000 of tax-free interest. It can only be used by company owners who have less than £5,000 of taxable *non-savings income* (typically salary income and rental income but not dividends).

The £5,000 starting rate band can usually only be enjoyed by company owners who take a small salary (typically no more than the £12,500 personal allowance) and have little or no rental income or other non-savings income.

It's also important to point out that both the £1,000 savings allowance and £5,000 starting rate band eat up your basic-rate band. They are not stand alone allowances.

The practical effect is that, if your company pays you £6,000 of tax-free interest, it's possible that £6,000 of your dividend income will be pushed over the higher-rate threshold where it will be taxed at 32.5% instead of 7.5%.

Borrowing to Lend to Your Company

If a company owner doesn't have spare savings to lend to the company they can borrow the money personally and lend it to their company.

Within certain fairly generous limits, the company owner can then claim tax relief for the interest paid to the bank against all of their taxable income (including their interest income or dividend income).

Summary

In summary, if a company owner sets up a small self-administered scheme (SSAS) they can use some of their pension savings to make a loan to their company.

This may be attractive if obtaining a conventional bank loan would be difficult or expensive.

There are costs involved when setting up and running a SSAS and arranging a loan.

There are also strict rules that have to be followed, although a reputable pension company will make sure these are all followed to the letter.

Part 8

The Self Employed & Property Investors

Chapter 35

Pension Planning for the Self Employed

The number of self-employed business owners saving for retirement has fallen dramatically in recent years.

Back in the 1990s around 60% were contributing to a pension. Today the figure is apparently closer to 25%.

When HMRC uses the term 'self employed' they are referring specifically to owners of unincorporated businesses, ie sole traders and partnerships. Most company owners are classified as employees (see Part 7 for more on company owners).

Most of the chapters in this guide are relevant for self-employed individuals. However, there are a few additional points that need to be made.

In particular, to maximise the tax relief on your pension contributions it is important to know how much taxable income you have. Most regular employees know how much taxable income they have: all they have to do is look at their payslips.

Many company owners also know how much taxable income they earn *personally*. The *company's* profits may fluctuate from year to year but many directors know how much salary or dividend income they are going to withdraw.

The taxable income of self-employed business owners is often much harder to predict. Taxable income for these individuals is normally the pre-tax profits of the business and there could be significant swings from year to year.

For example, a big order before the end of the tax year could increase taxable profits significantly. Several months of poor trading conditions could see profits fall sharply or even produce a loss for the year.

Sometimes it's not just the sales of the business that will result in big changes to taxable income. The business owner may deliberately drive down taxable profits, for example by making investments in tax-deductible equipment (e.g. vans or computers).

So what has all this got to do with maximising tax relief on pension contributions?

In Chapter 2 we pointed out that to enjoy any tax relief on your pension contributions you must have 'relevant UK earnings'. If your business makes a loss you won't have any earnings and the maximum pension contribution you can make is £3,600 (the 'universal pension contribution' that everyone under age 75 can make).

In Chapter 4 we pointed out that to maximise your higher-rate tax relief, your gross pension contributions should not exceed the amount of income you have over the higher-rate threshold (£50,000 in most parts of the UK, £43,430 in Scotland).

In other words, someone living in England with taxable income of £60,000, who wants to maximise their higher-rate tax relief, should make a gross pension contribution of no more than £10,000 (£60,000 – £50,000).

A sole trader with bumper profits of £90,000 may wish to make a big catch-up pension contribution of, say, £40,000 but suspend contributions if taxable profits fall below the higher-rate threshold.

In Chapter 17 we discussed the pros and cons of postponing pension contributions if you are a temporary basic-rate taxpayer. For example, during tough economic times (or if the business has a lot of tax-deductible expenditure for the year) the business owner may become a basic-rate taxpayer and decide to postpone making pension contributions until he becomes a higher-rate taxpayer in a future tax year.

Finally, in Chapter 19 we explained why self-employed business owners, who are the highest earners in households that receive child benefit, may wish to make bigger than normal pension contributions when their profits are £50,000 to £60,000. This will help them reduce or avoid the child benefit tax charge.

Calculating Pre-tax Profits

Although many sole traders may wish to vary the amount they contribute to a pension each year in order to maximise their tax relief, the problem for some is they don't know how much profit the business is making.

They may only have this information after they draw up their accounts for the year. This may happen many months after the tax year has ended – in other words, when it is too late to make pension contributions (remember you cannot make backdated pension contributions).

Example
Elliott is a sole trader with a 31 March year end.

On 5 April 2021 (the final day of the 2020/21 tax year) he makes a net cash pension contribution of £4,000. The taxman adds £1,000 of basic-rate tax relief to produce a gross pension contribution of £5,000. Elliott expects to have pre-tax profits of over £55,000 for 2020/21 and therefore expects to receive the maximum higher-rate tax relief of £1,000 (£5,000 x 20%).

Elliott's accountant finishes drawing up the accounts for the business in July 2021 and, after taking account of all of his tax-deductible expenditure, calculates that Elliott has pre-tax profits of £52,000.

This means Elliott will only enjoy higher-rate tax relief on £2,000 of his £5,000 gross pension contribution (£52,000 - £50,000 higher-rate threshold), saving him just £400 in higher-rate tax (£2,000 x 20%). If Elliott had known his profits would be lower than expected, he may have held onto some of his cash and made a bigger pension contribution in a future tax year when his income was higher.

The problem for Elliott is he had just five days from the end of his business accounting period to the end of the tax year to calculate his pre-tax profits and make a pension contribution that produced the maximum amount of higher-rate tax relief.

Most business owners would find this difficult if not impossible to do and very few accountants would work to such a tight deadline.

Some business owners have a 5th of April year end and therefore no time at all to accurately calculate their pre-tax profits.

Uncertainty about the level of pre-tax profits is less of a problem for business owners who are confident their pre-tax profits will exceed the higher-rate threshold by a significant margin, especially if their pension contributions are quite modest (for example, someone who reckons pre-tax profits will be £80,000 and wants to make a £5,000 pension contribution).

However, uncertainty about the level of pre-tax profits could be a problem for high earners who want to make big catch-up pension contributions and want higher-rate tax relief on the whole amount (for example, someone who expects to have pre-tax profits of £90,000 and wants to make a £40,000 pension contribution).

Changing the Accounting Year End

One option is to change your accounting year end to a date other than the tax year.

For example, let's say the business year end is 30 April 2020. This year end falls into the 2020/21 tax year which means the business owner would have from 30 April 2020 until the end of the tax year on 5 April 2021 to draw up accounts and decide what level of pension contribution to make.

Changing your accounting date has other tax benefits and drawbacks. For more information see the Taxcafe guide, *Small Business Tax Saving Tactics*.

Chapter 36

Pension Planning for Property Investors

When I started out writing this guide, I planned to conduct a comprehensive study comparing pensions and buy-to-let property. However, I quickly abandoned this idea for two reasons.

Firstly, a pension is not an asset, it's simply a 'wrapper' that protects the underlying assets from tax. Those assets are normally shares and bonds and sometimes commercial property (but not residential property which is prohibited).

So any comparison between pensions and buy-to-let ultimately boils down to a comparison between stock market investing and residential property investing.

Plenty of academics have conducted studies to see which asset class performs best but the results are sensitive to the time period under consideration and, critically, whether you include rents and dividends in the analysis.

The second reason why I decided not to spend time comparing pensions and buy-to-let property is that many property investors would simply not countenance investing in anything else. "Nothing beats bricks and mortar," goes the popular mantra.

I've lost count of the number of times I've heard the phrase "my properties are my pension".

So what I've decided to do in this chapter is explore whether a pension can be used to *complement* an investment in buy-to-let property.

This is particularly important now that tax relief on mortgage interest has been reduced.

Many landlords will see their tax bills rise significantly but it may be possible to mitigate the effects by making pension contributions.

Changes to Mortgage Tax Relief

Tax relief for interest and finance costs paid by individual landlords who own residential properties is now restricted.

The new rules do not apply to commercial properties or furnished holiday lettings or to properties held inside companies.

Tax relief was phased out over a period of four years and replaced with a 20% basic-rate "tax reduction" as follows:

- 2017/18   75% deducted as normal, 25% at basic rate only
- 2018/19   50% deducted as normal, 50% at basic rate only
- 2019/20   25% deducted as normal, 75% at basic rate only
- 2020/21   All relieved at basic rate only from this year on

The reduced tax relief on mortgage interest means many landlords will have significantly bigger *taxable* rental profits, even if their true rental profits remain unchanged.

Using Pensions to Beat the Tax Increase

A simple way for landlords to beat the tax increase is by making pension contributions.

How much will you need to invest to claw back all the extra tax you'll pay? As a rule of thumb, your *gross* pension contribution will need to be half as big as your mortgage interest.

So if you have £10,000 of buy-to-let interest you will typically need to make a gross pension contribution of £5,000 to recover the extra tax you will pay.

Example – Before Pension Contribution
In 2020/21 Usman earns £40,000 as a self-employed consultant and a rental profit of £10,000 (after deducting £10,000 of buy-to-let interest) from some residential properties. If Usman's mortgage tax relief was NOT restricted he would have total taxable income of £50,000 and his total after-tax income would be:

£50,000 income - £7,500 tax = £42,500

However, with his mortgage interest no longer tax deductible, Usman's income tax bill increases by £2,000 to £9,500 (he'll have an extra £10,000 taxed at 40% but will also be entitled to a 20% tax reduction). In summary, his after-tax income will fall from £42,500 to £40,500.

(Usman's national insurance has been ignored for simplicity.)

Example – After Pension Contribution
Usman decides to invest £4,000 in his pension. The taxman will add £1,000 of basic-rate tax relief, giving him a gross pension contribution of £5,000. He will also receive higher-rate tax relief through his self-assessment tax computation. This is calculated as 20% of his gross pension contribution: £5,000 x 20% = £1,000.

In total Usman enjoys £2,000 tax relief by making a £5,000 gross pension contribution (a cash contribution of £4,000). Hence, all the extra tax arising due to the reduction in his interest relief is clawed back by making a gross pension contribution half as big as his mortgage interest payments.

Pensions: Cashflow Issues

Although you can completely reverse the tax increase by making pension contributions, there is one significant problem: your money is locked away until you reach the minimum retirement age (currently 55). In other words, pension contributions can seriously damage your cashflow!

We saw that Usman's disposable income falls from £42,500 to £40,500 with his mortgage tax relief restricted. By making a pension contribution he claws back £2,000 and ends up with £42,500 again BUT £5,000 of that is stuck inside a pension plan! His actual disposable income will fall by a further £3,000 to £37,500. Usman's financial position is summarised below:

Usman: Tax Relief versus Cash Flow

	No Pension Contribution	Pension Contribution
	£	£
Sole trader profit	40,000	40,000
Taxable rental profit	20,000	20,000
	---------	---------
	60,000	60,000
Less:		
Income tax	9,500[1]	8,500[2]
Pension contribution	0	4,000
Mortgage interest[3]	10,000	10,000
Disposable income[4]	**40,500**	**37,500**
Pension Pot	**0**	**5,000**

Notes

1. First £12,500 tax free, next £37,500 taxed at 20%, final £10,000 taxed at 40%. Reduced by £2,000 tax reduction (mortgage interest x 20%).
2. Further reduced by £1,000 higher-rate tax relief on pension contribution.
3. Taxable rental profit is not the same as actual rental profit; his £10,000 of mortgage interest must be deducted to calculate his true disposable income.
4. Ignores national insurance payments. These would be the same under both scenarios and hence do not alter the overall conclusion.

Why does Usman's disposable income fall by £3,000? Because he personally invests £4,000 into his pension but gets £1,000 of higher-rate tax relief back through his self-assessment tax computation.

In summary, from 2020/21 onwards, for every £10,000 of mortgage interest you pay, you will generally be able to claw back the extra tax you face as a higher-rate taxpayer by making a £5,000 gross pension contribution. £3,000 will ultimately come from you and £2,000 from the taxman. Thus, your disposable income will also fall by a further £3,000.

Protecting Your Child Benefit

So far we've looked at the "bread and butter" case where the landlord is a regular higher-rate taxpayer and enjoys 40% tax relief on the pension contributions. Some landlords may be able to enjoy even more tax relief.

Take Usman, for example. His taxable income has risen from £50,000 (before the tax change) to £60,000 in 2020/21.

With income over £50,000 he will pay the child benefit charge if he is a parent and the highest earner in his household. In this case a pension contribution will reduce his "adjusted net income" which will also reduce the child benefit charge.

For example, a £5,000 gross pension contribution will reduce his adjusted net income from £60,000 to £55,000 which means his child benefit charge will be halved from £2,545 to £1,272 (if he has three children). In total, Usman will enjoy £3,273 tax relief on his £5,000 pension contribution, i.e. 65% tax relief.

Other Important Tax Thresholds

If your taxable income is pushed over the £100,000 threshold you will start losing your personal allowance. Once your income reaches £125,000 your personal allowance is completely withdrawn this year.

But making pension contributions reduces your adjusted net income which claws back some of your personal allowance. As a result, making pension contributions while your income is in the £100,000-£125,000 tax bracket will generally provide you with 60% tax relief.

If your taxable income gets pushed over the £150,000 tax threshold you will start paying additional rate tax at 45%. The flipside is you can enjoy up to 45% tax relief on any pension contributions you make.

Your annual allowance (the maximum amount that can be invested in your pension) may be reduced if your "adjusted income" exceeds £240,000 – See Chapter 20 for more information.

Do You Have Earnings?

Everyone under 75 can make a gross pension contribution of up to £3,600 per year.

If you want to contribute more your gross contributions must not exceed your annual earnings.

Salaries and trading profits are earnings for this purpose; rental profits generally are not. If a landlord wants to make big pension contributions he must have earnings from other sources.

Tax on Withdrawals

Apart from your 25% tax-free lump sum, withdrawals from your pension pot will be fully taxed.

Ultimately, therefore, pension contributions cannot completely reverse the increase in your income tax bill caused by the restriction to mortgage tax relief.

However, with proper timing, you may be able to minimise the tax on your withdrawals and make sure that some of them are tax free or taxed at no more than 20%.

Chapter 37

Putting Property into a Pension

Some business owners use a specialist SIPP or other pension plan to hold their business premises and in this chapter we'll take a look at the benefits and drawbacks.

Note that you can put *commercial property* into a pension but not residential property, so this option is not available to buy-to-let landlords.

Holding business property in a pension has a number of benefits:

- **Tax-free rent**. There is no income tax payable by you on the rent your business pays into your pension plan. These rent payments are also a tax deductible expense for the business.

- **No capital gains tax**. When a property held inside a pension is sold there is no capital gains tax payable.

- **Inheritance tax exemption**. Assets held in a pension fall outside your estate for inheritance tax purposes.

Although the ability to roll up rental income tax free inside a pension is enticing, you must never lose sight of the fact that all the money you eventually withdraw from your pension, over and above your 25% tax-free lump sum, will be subject to income tax.

If you are a higher-rate taxpayer at present but expect to be a basic-rate taxpayer when you retire (most retirees end up as basic-rate taxpayers), it's possible the rental income will ultimately be much less heavily taxed by going the pension route.

Similarly, although property held inside a pension can be sold without incurring capital gains tax, when you eventually withdraw the capital gain most of it (75%) will be subject to income tax.

If you are a basic-rate taxpayer when you retire you will pay 20% tax and if you are a higher-rate taxpayer you will pay 40% tax.

By contrast, if you sell commercial property that you own personally you will be subject to capital gains tax. Commercial property now benefits from the lower 20% CGT rate and it's possible some of the gain will be taxed at just 10% if your basic-rate band isn't used up by your other income. Some of the gain may also be covered by your annual exemption, currently £12,300.

In some cases a sale of business premises owned personally will qualify for Entrepreneurs Relief. If so, a tax rate of 10% may apply to the whole gain, although this will generally not be the case if your company has paid you rent at a full commercial rate.

Business premises held inside your pension do not have to be sold when you retire. If your own business ceases to occupy the property, the property can remain in your pension and be rented out to someone else and the rent will roll up tax free in your pension.

Although property held inside your pension may fall outside your estate for inheritance tax purposes, in most cases the family members that inherit your pension pot will have to pay income tax on any money they subsequently withdraw, typically at 20% or 40%.

By contrast, if you own your business premises personally, the property may qualify for business property relief (100% if you are a sole trader, 50% if the business is used by your partnership or company).

Finally, when it comes to tucking away money inside a pension we must never lose sight of the fact that you will not be able to get your hands on any of the money until you are at least 55 (probably rising to 57 in 2028).

Clearly there are benefits to holding business property inside a pension but it is by no means a 'no brainer'. There are benefits but also drawbacks and each case would have to be decided on its merits with help from a professional.

Funding the Property Purchase

The purchase of a business property by a pension can be funded in several ways.

Typically you will use your existing pension savings, topped up with fresh contributions (including company pension contributions if you run a company).

It is also possible for your pension fund to borrow money but only up to 50% of its net assets. For example, if you have pension savings of £100,000 an additional £50,000 can be borrowed.

Some pension providers allow a part share in a property to be acquired by the pension plan, with the balance owned outside the pension.

Several individuals can also pool their pension savings to collectively buy a property.

Transferring Existing Property

If you already own the property you can sell it to your SIPP and this may allow you to release a sizeable amount of cash from your pension savings.

Transferring an existing property into a pension is likely to result in capital gains tax becoming payable if the property has risen in value since you bought it.

As stated earlier, commercial property now benefits from the lower 20% CGT rate and some of the gain may be taxed at just 10% and some may be tax-free thanks to the annual exemption. It is unlikely Entrepreneurs Relief would be available in such cases.

A sizeable capital gains tax bill may put off many existing property owners going down the pension route but others may still be tempted by the prospect of receiving a large cash payment out of their pension savings.

The transfer may also result in a stamp duty land tax bill and VAT may also be payable in certain circumstances, although a refund can usually be claimed.

In Specie Contributions

Properties have also been transferred into pensions as *in specie* pension contributions, with the member claiming income tax relief. Under this method a property worth, say, £100,000 would be transferred into the pension scheme with the pension scheme administrator claiming £25,000 of basic-rate tax relief to add to the member's pension pot and the member himself claiming up to £25,000 of higher-rate tax relief when he submitted his tax return.

In specie contributions are not permitted by most pension firms following a clamp down by HMRC because of perceived abuse. However, in a recent First-tier Tribunal decision it was decided to allow tax relief on an in specie contribution of shares. HMRC has appealed this decision but at the time of writing the outcome of the appeal was still awaited.

Costs and other Formalities

Not all pension providers deal with property purchases so you may need to transfer your existing pension savings to a specialist provider.

When your property is held inside a pension your business will have to be treated just like any other tenant, with no special favours, which means rent will have to be paid at a full market rate come hell or high water.

If rent is not paid this will be treated as an unauthorised payment by your SIPP and HMRC may levy a charge of 40% on you personally and a charge of up to 40% on the SIPP itself.

Property SIPPs are also much more expensive to run than those that only allow you to invest in traditional 'stocks and shares'.

Initial set up costs include legal fees, surveyor fees, lenders fees and fees to the pension company managing your SIPP.

Fees will have to be paid for regular rent revaluations and a third party property manager may have to be appointed to collect the rent from you.

Part 9

Family Pension Planning

Chapter 38

Couples: Who Should Make the Pension Contributions?

People without earnings (i.e. who don't work) can make a pension contribution of £2,880 per year. The taxman will add £720 of basic-rate tax relief, resulting in a gross pension contribution of £3,600.

Is this worth doing?

Some people think it is because, although there will only be basic-rate tax relief, the ultimate pension income may end up being completely tax free, covered by the individual's income tax personal allowance.

The broader question that needs answering is this:

Under what circumstances should you transfer money to a spouse or partner to make pension contributions?

We can answer this question with the aid of a case study.

Case Study

Rory is a higher-rate taxpayer and his wife Claire is either a basic-rate taxpayer or doesn't work at all (whichever you prefer). Rory contributes to a pension, Claire doesn't. The couple want to make additional pension contributions and are trying to decide *who* should make them.

Rory will enjoy higher-rate tax relief on his extra pension contributions BUT he expects to ultimately pay 20% income tax on his pension income. Claire will only enjoy basic-rate tax relief on her pension contributions BUT she hopes to pay 0% tax on her pension income (being fully covered by her personal allowance).

Let's assume the couple want to save an additional £2,880 annually. If Claire makes the contributions the taxman will add £720 of basic-rate tax relief, producing a gross pension contribution of £3,600.

Rory can make a net cash contribution of £3,840. The taxman will add £960 of basic-rate relief, resulting in a gross contribution of £4,800. Rory will also receive £960 of higher-rate tax relief (£4,800 x 20%), so the net cost to him is also £2,880 (£3,840 - £960).

Every year Rory has an extra £4,800 going into his pension, whereas Claire only has £3,600.

If the money grows by 7% per year then after 20 years Rory's additional contributions will have grown to £210,553, whereas Claire will have £157,915.

In summary, Rory ends up with 33% more money than Claire... but this is no real surprise (see Chapter 17).

Withdrawing Income

Let's say they pass the minimum retirement age and decide to withdraw money from their pensions.

They can both take a 25% tax-free lump sum. The remaining 75% will be taxed when withdrawn.

Their positions are summarised in Table 7. The total after tax includes the tax-free lump sum and the income remaining after paying tax at either 0%, 20% or 40%.

For example, if Rory's additional contributions have grown to £210,553 he will be able to take a tax-free lump sum of £52,638. If the remaining £157,915 is taxed at 20% he will be left with after-tax income of £126,332 – £178,970 in total.

Of course, Rory won't be able to withdraw the whole £157,915 in one tax year and pay just 20% tax – he will have to spread his withdrawals over several tax years.

The example is simplistic but does offer very interesting insights.

Table 7
Couples Pension Planning
Who Should Make Contributions?

	Higher-rate relief on contributions	Basic-rate relief on contributions
	£	£
Total pension pot	210,553	157,915
25% Tax-free	52,638	39,479
75% Taxable	157,915	118,436
Total after tax:		
After-tax @ 0%	210,553	157,915
After-tax @ 20%	178,970	134,228
After-tax @ 40%	147,387	110,541

When Rory Should Make the Contributions

If Rory pays 20% income tax when he retires (remember he has other pension savings) he will end up with £178,970 eventually. If Claire pays 0% income tax (because she has no other pension savings and her pension withdrawals are covered by her income tax personal allowance over several tax years) she will end up with £157,915. Rory ends up with 13% more money.

So the first conclusion is this: Rory should keep on making the pension contributions, even if Claire's pension income will be tax free.

It's even more important that Rory makes the contributions if there is any likelihood that Claire will acquire another source of income (e.g. from rental properties, inherited assets, a business or job etc). If Claire ends up being taxed at 20% on her pension income she may end up with £134,228 to Rory's £178,970. Rory ends up with 33% more money in this scenario.

When Claire Should Make the Contributions

But what if Rory, like Claire, does not receive higher-rate tax relief on these additional pension contributions, only basic-rate tax relief? This would be the case if his existing pension contributions are already equal to the amount of income he has taxed at 40% (see Chapter 4 for an explanation).

In this case Rory would end up with £134,228 to Claire's £157,915. Claire receives 18% more income in this scenario.

So the second conclusion is this: Claire should make the additional contributions if Rory cannot obtain any additional higher-rate tax relief and she expects to pay no tax on her pension income. It's a second-best outcome but may be the best route for some couples.

If Rory expects to be a higher-rate taxpayer when he retires (e.g. if he has a lot of other pension savings or taxable income) he could end up with £147,387. Claire will end up with £157,915 but only if she pays no tax on her pension withdrawals. If she pays 20% tax she will end up worse off than Rory, even though he pays 40% tax.

In most cases Claire only ends up better off than Rory if she pays 0% tax on her pension income. However, if she works she will eventually receive a taxable state pension which will probably use up a significant chunk of her personal allowance which means she will pay 20% tax on most of her other pension income.

Even if Claire has never worked she may receive some state pension. For example, she will build up state pension entitlement while she has children under 12 and qualifies for child benefit.

In these cases Claire may only be able to pay 0% tax on all her pension income if all her pension savings are withdrawn before she reaches state pension age. This may only be possible if she has a relatively small pension pot.

Less Common Scenarios

There are other permutations, including Rory paying 0% tax when he retires (the best-case scenario of all) and Claire paying 40% tax when she retires (the worst-case scenario of all) but these outcomes are less likely and will not be discussed further.

Avoiding the Child Benefit Charge

If Claire receives child benefit and Rory's taxable income is in the £50,000-£60,000 bracket, he should probably be the one making all the pension contributions.

This will allow him to reduce or avoid the child benefit tax charge and enjoy over 50% tax relief on his pension contributions (see Chapter 19).

Family Tax Planning and Other Issues

Finally, it's worth pointing out that Claire may have *non-tax* reasons for making pension contributions, for example if she feels this gives her greater financial security.

On this note it should be pointed out that there are other things the couple can do to make use of Claire's tax-free personal allowance before she receives any state pension. For example, rental properties and other assets could be placed in her name, as could money the couple may eventually inherit.

Lifetime ISAs

These are discussed in detail in Part 3. Those under 40 can save up to £4,000 per year in a Lifetime ISA with a £1,000 Government bonus.

If Claire is under 40 she may prefer to put her money into a Lifetime ISA instead of a pension because the upfront tax relief is the same BUT all her withdrawals will be completely tax free.

Similarly, if Rory expects to be a higher-rate taxpayer when he retires he may be better off investing his additional savings in a Lifetime ISA.

Chapter 39

Pensions for Children and Grandchildren

"When I was a boy of 14, my father was so ignorant I could hardly stand to have the old man around. But when I got to be 21, I was astonished at how much the old man had learned in seven years."
Mark Twain

Everyone under the age of 75 can make a pension contribution of £3,600 per year and receive basic-rate tax relief (which reduces the net cost to £2,880).

This means minor children can make pension contributions or, as is more likely in practice, their parents or grandparents can contribute on their behalf.

Many pension providers have special pension plans for minors, like the Junior SIPP from Hargreaves Lansdown. According to HM Revenue and Customs, around 60,000 children under 18 years of age are making use of this tax break.

Making pension contributions on behalf of a minor child could be a wonderful way to leave an asset of lasting value that cannot be frittered away, at least not until the child is a responsible adult!

These contributions have the added bonus of usually being exempt from inheritance tax, being covered by either the £3,000 annual exemption or the regular gifts out of income exemption.

A pension contribution made on behalf of a minor child could grow into a significant nest egg. For example, let's say you make 18 annual contributions of £2,880 starting in the year a child is born. Each contribution will be topped up with £720 of basic-rate tax relief (even though the child doesn't pay any income tax), producing a gross pension contribution of £3,600 per year.

If we assume that the investments in the pension grow by 7% per year, just before the child's 18th birthday, when the last contribution is made, the pension pot will be worth £122,397. However, that's not the end of the story. The money will continue to compound tax free until the child reaches the minimum retirement age. For example, when the child is 58 the pension pot could be worth close to £2 million.

Of course these figures aren't adjusted for inflation. If some inflation adjustments are made you still end up with a pension pot worth over £350,000 in today's money, which is still a tidy sum!

We don't know what the minimum retirement age will be many decades from now – it could be a lot higher than 58 – and that is perhaps one major drawback of contributing to a pension so early.

Junior ISAs

Just like normal ISAs, money grows tax free but there is no upfront tax relief, as there is with pension contributions.

The annual investment limit was raised to £9,000 from 6 April 2020.

Unlike regular ISAs, money cannot be withdrawn until the child reaches age 18. From that date the junior ISA becomes an adult ISA and the child can do what he or she likes with the money.

Junior SIPP vs Junior ISA

There's no doubt most children or grandchildren would prefer you to contribute to a junior ISA instead of a junior SIPP. They will face big financial commitments between the age of 18 and retirement age: university fees, mortgages, childcare costs etc.

However, there is a risk that the child will fritter away all of that carefully saved money if they can access it at the tender age of 18.

Personally I prefer the pension route for the simple reason that your children or grandchildren will have to save for retirement anyway. In other words, they can never lose out with a pension but they can lose out with a junior ISA that is not spent wisely.

They'll thank you for it… one day!

Part 10

Pension Planning and the Coronavirus Crisis

Chapter 40

Withdrawing Money from Your Pension

At present you can access your private pension savings when you reach age 55.

According to HMRC, £2.5 billion was withdrawn from pensions under the pension freedom rules in the first three months of 2020, a 19% increase over the same period in 2019.

A total of 348,000 individuals withdrew money from their pensions, a 23% increase over the same period in 2019. The average withdrawal was £7,100.

HMRC only receives information on *taxable* payments. Tax-free payments (such as tax-free lump sums) are not included in the above statistics.

These figures do not show the full impact of the coronavirus crisis, which only started to affect the economy in the second half of March 2020 (in other words, during the last couple of weeks of the three month period).

It is very likely that there will be far larger than normal pension withdrawals in the months ahead, as many individuals struggle with redundancy, reduced pay or depressed business conditions.

So what are the benefits and drawbacks of withdrawing money from your pension to help you through these difficult times?

Beware of Pension Scams

The first important point to make is that you cannot access your pension savings at all before you are 55, unless you are suffering from "ill health" or "serious ill health" (see Chapter 7).

Since the introduction of pension freedom in 2015 there have been numerous firms peddling schemes that purport to "unlock" your pension before age 55. A common term for these schemes is "pension liberation".

They are almost always scams.

All manner of financial fraud has been on the increase since the onset of the coronavirus crisis. Action Fraud reported a 400% increase in coronavirus-related scams in March 2020, with losses totalling almost £1 million.

The Pension Regulator and the Financial Conduct Authority (FCA) have been urging pension savers not to make rash decisions with their pension savings. They fear that criminals are seeking to exploit fears over stock market turmoil, encouraging people to invest their savings in "safe" investments with "guaranteed returns".

There are also concerns that those who are under 55 and struggling to make ends meet will be lured into scams that promise early access to pension savings.

Pension liberation scams often lure victims with offers of a "free pension review". This is then accompanied by high pressure sales tactics. Cold calling has been commonplace but these days scammers are also using social media to find new victims.

The pension liberation scam typically operates by getting the victim to transfer his or her existing pension pot to a small self-administered scheme (SSAS). This type of pension scheme can be registered online with HMRC relatively easily, giving the whole set up the appearance of legitimacy.

Small self-administered schemes are normally used by small limited companies, so the scammers will also register a company with you as a director. The company will usually remain dormant and never trade.

A huge fee will be charged for making the initial pension transfer (perhaps 30% of your pension pot) and the scammers will then charge huge commissions for investing your money. These 'investments' may be in the scammers own companies... or your savings may simply be stolen outright.

The scam is dressed up as "pension liberation" because the victim will typically be offered a loan or cash back out of their pension savings (with a promise that it doesn't have to be repaid). The victim may also be offered a cut of investment commissions.

To add insult to injury, when the victim has detected the scam, they may be contacted by the fraudsters a second time, pretending to be a claims company and offering to recoup their losses for a fee!

And if you think losing all your pension savings to scammers is bad enough, any money you receive out of your pension savings before age 55 is likely to be treated as an unauthorised payment and HMRC will levy a tax charge of at least 55% on the amount withdrawn.

Fortunately, the authorities and the pensions industry have been clamping down on pension liberation scams, with new legislation and a pension industry code of good practice to make it more difficult to transfer pension pots to bogus pension schemes.

However, fraudsters always manage to stay one step ahead of the law, so the easiest way to protect your pension savings is to never respond to any call, email or advert promising you access to your pension savings before age 55.

Pension Scams and the Over 55s

Individuals who are 55 or older are a much easier target for pension fraudsters because they are allowed to withdraw all of their pension savings and can do what they like with them.

Once you withdraw your pension savings it's a lot harder for the pension watchdogs and regulators to prevent your money falling into the hands of crooks.

With many pension savers worried about plunging share prices, the coronavirus crisis has created a happy hunting ground for scammers offering "safe" investments or investments with "guaranteed returns".

These investments are often overseas and unregulated with no consumer protection. They will often use complicated investment structures and be packaged as long term – so that victims do not realise they have been duped for a number of years.

According to the Pension Regulator, the investments will often appear quite exotic – for example, overseas property and hotels, forestry, vineyards and renewable energy.

The investments are often worthless or do not even exist. Even if the offer is not a scam as such, the investments will probably be unregulated and high risk and involve putting all your eggs into one basket.

Again, the simplest way to protect yourself from a scam or dodgy investment is to ignore any type of investment solicitation, whether by phone, email, social media or advertising.

The Long-term Cost of Early Withdrawals

Once you reach age 55 you can withdraw as much money as you like from your pension. Those facing financial hardship because of the coronavirus crisis may be considering making a withdrawal from their pension savings for the first time.

There is, however, no escaping the fact that any withdrawal before your planned retirement age means you will:

- Have less income when you eventually retire, or
- Have to retire later, or
- Have to fill the hole with bigger contributions in future

These problems may be magnified if you withdraw money while the economic shock from the coronavirus crisis still weighs heavily on financial markets.

To withdraw money from your pension you may have to sell stock market investments that have fallen significantly in value, before they've had sufficient time to recover. In other words, the timing probably couldn't be worse.

Even if you don't withdraw any money from your pension at present, the fallout from the coronavirus crisis means that many pension savers will probably have to make bigger contributions in the future or accept a smaller retirement income or work longer.

This is unless the investments held inside those pensions recover very strongly, something that is by no means certain.

Example
Before the coronavirus crisis hit the world's financial markets Marion had a pension pot worth £150,000 which has now fallen in value to £100,000. She doesn't withdraw any money from her pension during the crisis. If her investments then grow by 7% per year it will take a whole six years before those savings have recovered their lost ground.

This example shows that even those who leave their pension pots intact may not escape the fallout from the coronavirus crisis.

Example
Her husband Glen also had a pension pot worth £150,000 which has now fallen in value to £100,000. Because he is over 55 he decides to withdraw his tax-free lump sum (£25,000) to keep his business going. This leaves him with just £75,000 in his pension. If his investments then grow by 7% per year, after six years he will have just £112,500 and will have to find an additional £37,500 to plug the gap and catch up with Marion. Alternatively he will have to wait 10 years before his pension pot has recovered the ground lost during the coronavirus crisis.

Tax-Free Lump Sums

If you do decide to tap your pension early the least damaging thing you can do is withdraw no more than your 25% tax-free lump sum.

It's important to remember that you don't have to withdraw your whole tax-free lump sum. In Chapter 8 we saw how you can use something called phased drawdown to withdraw just a small tax-free lump sum.

An example in that chapter showed how someone called Stacey was able to take just £10,000 tax free out of her £200,000 pension pot. She did this by transferring £40,000 into a flexi-access drawdown plan and withdrawing just the 25% tax-free lump sum of £10,000. She was able to leave the remaining £30,000 in the drawdown plan without taking any additional taxable income.

Taxable Withdrawals

Once you have withdrawn your entire 25% tax-free lump sum any further withdrawals will be fully taxed.

That in itself is not necessarily a bad thing. If your income has fallen sharply during the current tax year and is well below £50,000, any income you withdraw from your pension will be taxed at just 20%. Some of it may even be tax free if covered by your personal allowance.

If you make a big withdrawal it's possible some of it will be taxed at 40% and there may be other penalties, such as the loss of your income tax personal allowance.

However, tax is not usually the main problem when it comes to withdrawing income from your pension early. As we saw in Chapter 8, if you withdraw just £1 of taxable income from your pension your ability to make any further pension contributions may be permanently curtailed.

You may become subject to something called the money purchase annual allowance which allows you to make a pension contribution of just £4,000 per year... forever. This is the maximum gross contribution, with £3,200 coming from you and £800 from the taxman.

If you are subject to the money purchase annual allowance you also cannot carry forward any unused allowance from previous tax years.

Such a small contribution may not be a problem if you have already built up a big enough pension pot. For anyone else it's a disaster.

Example
Gerry is 55 and has a pension pot worth £200,000. Because his business has been so severely affected by the coronavirus crisis he decides to withdraw a tax-free lump sum of £50,000. Later in the year he's forced to withdraw a further £25,000 to keep the business going. This second withdrawal will be subject to income tax and trigger the money purchase annual allowance.

Gerry had always planned to make big contributions close to retirement and hoped to build a pension pot worth £500,000. Now he is restricted to making a contribution of just £4,000 per year. Contributions of £4,000 per year which, when invested, grow by 7% per year will be worth just £59,000 after 10 years.

Thanks to the stingy money purchase annual allowance, Gerry isn't able to plug the gap caused by his coronavirus crisis withdrawals, let alone build a pension pot worth £500,000.

Loans for Business Purposes

As we saw in Chapter 34, if a company owner transfers his pension savings to a small self-administered scheme (SSAS), a loan of up to 50% of the pension scheme's assets can be made to the company.

A pension loan may be attractive if obtaining conventional bank funding is difficult or expensive.

However, there are many costs involved when setting up and running a SSAS and for arranging a loan and these costs are by no means trivial.

And even though you would be lending *your* pension savings to *your* company, there are very strict rules that have to be followed – otherwise you will be subject to an unauthorised payment charge. For example, just like any bank loan, a pension loan must be repaid in regular instalments.

Apparently demand to open small self-administered schemes has rocketed since the onset of the coronavirus crisis, as struggling business owners seek to take advantage of the loan facility.

Personally I'm not convinced that anyone should set up a SSAS for the sole purpose of taking a business loan. In Chapter 34 we saw that company owners are only better off borrowing from their pensions if the interest rate charged by the bank is higher than the return they can earn on their pension investments.

It may also be impossible to obtain a pension loan at short notice if your company does not already have a SSAS set up. HMRC has to approve the registration of the new pension scheme and this will take time.

Bounce Back Loans

For businesses that need a loan it is worth pointing out that the Government has launched a new Bounce Back Loans Scheme as part of its huge package of business support during the coronavirus crisis:

gov.uk/guidance/apply-for-a-coronavirus-bounce-back-loan

Loans range from £2,000 to up to 25% of turnover. The maximum loan amount is £50,000.

The business must derive more than 50% of its income from trading activities (so property rental businesses will not qualify).

The Government has promised that cash can be accessed within days using this scheme.

The Government will provide lenders with a 100% guarantee and cover the cost of any fees and interest for the borrower for the first 12 months. The borrower does not have to make any repayments for the first 12 months.

Interest is charged at a flat rate of 2.5%. The length of the loan is 6 years but early repayment is allowed without any early repayment penalties.

Lenders are not allowed to take any form of personal guarantee or take recovery action over a borrower's personal assets (such as their main home).

The loans are easy to apply for using a short online application which contains just seven questions.

Chapter 41

Postponing Pension Contributions

Preserving Your Cash

As we've shown throughout this guide, pensions are a wonderful way to save for retirement and in many cases a much more powerful tax shelter than ISAs.

As we saw in Chapter 15, if you are a higher-rate taxpayer while you are making contributions and a basic-rate taxpayer when you retire (most retirees are basic-rate taxpayers), you could end up with at least 41.67% more income by saving through a pension instead of an ISA.

However, the problem with pensions is your money is locked up until you reach age 55 (possibly rising to 57 in 2028).

More than once in this guide I have stated that, if you're under 55, before making significant pension contributions you should make sure you have other resources to protect against:

* Unforeseen expenses, and an
* Unforeseen drop in income.

For many individuals the coronavirus crisis has resulted in an unforeseen drop in income. Anyone worried about the state of their finances may therefore wish to consider reducing or halting their pension contributions for a while.

Although this may result in a higher tax bill during the current tax year, most people will be able to completely reverse this tax increase by making bigger contributions in future tax years.

Even if you're 55 or older you cannot get your hands on all your pension contributions immediately without incurring a penalty. You can withdraw 25% as a tax free lump sum but anything more may trigger the money purchase annual allowance, which will limit your future pension contributions to just £4,000 per year forever.

So if you're 55 or older and worried about your current cash position you may also wish to consider reducing or halting your pension contributions for a while.

Reducing or halting your pension contributions does not mean you have to stop saving. There are lots of places you can put your savings and a pension is just one of them. An ISA is the obvious alternative.

In Chapter 18 it was shown that, if you want to retain immediate access to your savings, you do not have to put your money into a pension until you are ready.

We saw how Ian was able to put his savings into an ISA for several years and then stick those savings into a pension. He ended up with exactly the same amount of money in his pension as Peter, who had been making pension contributions the whole time.

In the meantime Ian had instant access to his savings, something that is important when the economic outlook is highly uncertain.

It was also pointed out that there are some risks and practical issues when it comes to postponing pension contributions.

For example:

- If higher-rate tax relief is scrapped to pay for the coronavirus crisis it will be impossible for higher-rate taxpayers to make up ground lost from postponing pension contributions (see Chapter 42).

- If you belong to a workplace pension scheme to which your employer is contributing, postponing your own contributions could prove costly: you will lose the free cash being offered by your employer.

- In order to enjoy higher-rate tax relief on a future catch-up contribution of, say, £20,000, you will need to have at least £20,000 of income taxed at 40%. If the higher-rate threshold is £50,000 this means having total taxable income of at least £70,000. If your income is not high enough, one solution is to spread your catch-up contributions over several tax years to maximise your higher-rate tax relief.

- The bigger your catch-up contribution, the more likely you are to exceed the annual allowance. The annual allowance is currently £40,000 but could be reduced in the years ahead (see Chapter 42). Fortunately, it is possible to carry forward any unused annual allowance from the three previous tax years. So if you don't make any pension contributions during the current tax year, you may be able to make a contribution of at least £80,000 next year.

Protecting Higher-Rate Tax Relief

Another reason why it may be a good idea to reduce or postpone your pension contributions is to protect your higher-rate tax relief if you expect your income to fall during the current tax year.

For the current 2020/21 tax year, if your taxable income is more than £50,000 you can enjoy higher-rate tax relief on your pension contributions. If your income is less than £50,000 all you will get is basic-rate tax relief.

Pensions are very attractive retirement saving vehicles if you enjoy higher-rate tax relief on your contributions. As we saw in Chapter 15, a higher-rate taxpayer could end up with at least 41.67% more income by saving through a pension instead of an ISA. But how do pensions and ISAs compare if you only receive basic-rate tax relief on your pension contributions?

Example
Ian and Peter are both basic-rate taxpayers and have £1,000 to invest. Ian puts his £1,000 in an ISA. Peter puts his £1,000 in a pension where the taxman adds £250 of basic-rate tax relief, giving him a total pension investment of £1,250.

We can ignore the growth on these investments over many years. Because both ISAs and pensions allow your investments to grow tax free there is no difference in the ultimate outcome. We can also ignore any additional money they decide to invest because that does not affect the comparison in any way either.

When Ian retires he can withdraw all of his £1,000 ISA saving tax free. Peter can withdraw 25% tax free (£312.50) and we will assume he pays 20% tax on the remaining £937.50, producing a tax bill of £187.50. After paying tax Peter is left with £1062.50 which is just 6.25% more than Ian.

This example reveals that:

If you make pension contributions when you are a basic-rate taxpayer and pay basic-rate tax on the income you withdraw, you will end up with just 6.25% more income than someone who uses an ISA to save.

We have assumed that Peter pays 20% tax on all the income he withdraws from his pension. It's possible some of the income will be tax free thanks to his income tax personal allowance, making a pension more attractive than this example would suggest.

Pensions are not quite so unattractive to all basic-rate taxpayers. If you belong to a workplace pension your employer will be contributing as well and in some schemes these contributions are very generous. Your employer may match the contribution you are making, thereby doubling the amount saved each month.

And if you belong to a salary sacrifice scheme you may be enjoying a national insurance saving as well (see Part 6).

Nevertheless, many basic-rate taxpayers do not have enough incentive to put their savings in a locked box until they are 55 (possibly rising to 57 in 2028), especially if they are many years away from reaching the minimum retirement age.

If you think you will be a basic-rate taxpayer this year but expect to be a higher-rate taxpayer in the future you may be better off postponing your pension contributions until then.

In Chapter 17 it was shown that if a basic-rate taxpayer postpones making pension contributions until they become a higher-rate taxpayer they could end up with 33% more retirement income.

Example
Matt is a sole trader who expects to make a pre-tax profit of £40,000 this year, much lower than normal. If he invests £4,000 in his pension the taxman will add £1,000 of basic-rate relief. But because Matt is not a higher-rate taxpayer he will not enjoy any higher-rate relief.

Let's say next year the higher-rate threshold is £50,000 again and Matt expects to have a pre-tax profit of £60,000. If he invests £4,000 in his pension the taxman will add £1,000 of basic-rate relief, resulting in a gross pension contribution of £5,000.

Because Matt is now a higher-rate taxpayer he can also claim £1,000 of higher-rate tax relief, found by multiplying his gross pension contribution by 20%:

$$£5,000 \text{ x } 20\% = £1,000$$

This example reminds us that higher-rate taxpayers enjoy twice as much tax relief on their pension contributions as basic-rate taxpayers.

If Matt postpones making pension contributions this year (when only basic-rate relief is available), he can catch up by making an <u>additional</u> gross contribution of £5,000 next year – £10,000 in total. He will enjoy full higher-rate tax relief on all of his contributions.

An added benefit of postponing his pension contribution is that, if Matt is the highest earner in a household claiming child benefit, he will completely avoid the child benefit charge next year. This is because his £10,000 gross pension contribution will reduce his adjusted net income from £60,000 to £50,000 (see Chapter 19).

How Much Can You Contribute with Higher-Rate Relief?

Even if your taxable income has fallen sharply because of the coronavirus crisis you may still end up with more than £50,000, meaning that you will still be a higher-rate taxpayer this year and can enjoy higher-rate tax relief on pension contributions.

However, you can only enjoy higher-rate tax relief to the extent that you have income taxed at 40%.

The maximum you can contribute with full higher-rate relief is:

Your taxable income <u>minus</u> the higher-rate threshold

For example, if your taxable income is £55,000 and the higher-rate threshold is £50,000 the maximum contribution you can make with full higher-rate tax relief is £5,000. This is your maximum *gross* pension contribution (which includes the taxman's top up). Multiply this number by 0.8 to obtain the maximum amount you invest personally: £4,000.

Sandy in the above example will be claiming the maximum higher-rate tax relief when he makes his catch-up contribution next year. If his contributions were any larger he would only enjoy basic-rate tax relief on the excess.

If you're making bigger than normal catch-up contributions its important to check that you will receive higher-rate tax relief on the whole amount.

The higher-rate threshold is £43,430 in Scotland, so anyone with taxable income over £43,430 can enjoy higher-rate tax relief.

Fear of Missing Out

Many financial advisors would argue that, with the stock market having fallen sharply in recent months, now is the wrong time to halt your pension contributions. Instead you should be drip feeding money into the stock market to take advantage of some of the "bargains" on offer. They may be right or they may be wrong. We have no idea where the stock market is heading in the months of years ahead (and neither do they).

It's important to remember that there are other ways to save and invest without locking up your money in a pension. For example, if you have not already used up your £20,000 ISA allowance you could stick your retirement savings in an ISA, enjoy tax-free income and capital gains, and later on put the money into your pension with full tax relief.

However, most financial advisers would agree that you should not be investing money in risky assets if you think you may need the money to cover your living costs in the short term.

Regular Salaried Employees

Not everyone should consider reducing or halting their pension contributions. If you belong to a workplace pension scheme to which your employer is also contributing, opting out could prove costly: you will also lose out on the contribution your employer is making, which could be significantly larger than your own.

Employees can opt out of their employers' workplace pension schemes at any time, although most would advise against this.

Company Owners

As explained in Chapter 32, pension contributions are an extremely tax efficient way to extract money from your company. When you retire you may be able to pay tax on your pension income at an effective rate of just 15%, compared with the overall tax rate of 25% or 45% you may currently be paying on your dividend income.

Company owners often get their companies to make pension contributions on their behalf because this is slightly more tax efficient than making them personally. Furthermore, many company owners only pay themselves a small salary and can therefore only make a small pension contribution personally. Contributions made by you personally must not exceed your annual earnings (i.e. your salary).

Pension contributions made by a company are not restricted by the level of the director's earnings. A company pension contribution can be a lot bigger than the director's earnings. There are, however, other restrictions and the company may be denied corporation tax relief on any pension contribution that is viewed as 'excessive', although this is fairly rare in practice.

Although pension contributions are an extremely tax efficient way to extract money from your company, anyone concerned about their company's cash position in the current climate may wish to consider reducing or halting their company pension contributions for a period.

Although this may result in a higher corporation tax bill for the company's current accounting period, it should be possible to completely reverse this tax increase by making bigger contributions in future years.

Reducing pension contributions may also make it easier to pay yourself dividend income in the near future, rather than having to pay yourself a much more heavily taxed salary or resort to borrowing money from your company.

A company must have sufficient distributable profits to pay dividends. Pension contributions reduce a company's taxable profit, which means there will be less after-tax profit to distribute as dividends.

Maximising Dividends Taxed at 7.5%

Those who benefit most from company pension contributions are higher-rate taxpayers. A company pension contribution that will one day be taxed at possibly just 15% is a lot more attractive from a tax saving standpoint than a dividend taxed at an overall rate of 45%.

Basic-rate taxpayers (those with income under £50,000 this year) pay tax at an overall effective rate of just 25% on their dividend income, compared with the 15% they may pay on their future pension income. So putting money in a locked box for many years is much less appealing to them.

If your taxable income this year is expected to be less than £50,000 and you have concerns about locking away cash in a pension scheme, it may be better to instead pay yourself more dividend income taxed at just 7.5%. The extra dividend income can always be lent back to the company if the company needs the money later on.

Making Bigger than Normal Contributions

From a tax saving standpoint some people may be better off continuing with their pension contributions or making bigger than normal contributions this year... if they have the spare cash to do so.

Protecting Your Child Benefit

If your taxable income is normally significantly higher than £60,000 but you expect it to fall back closer to £60,000 this year, you may be able to enjoy above average levels of tax relief on any pension contributions you make this year.

This is because income that falls into the £50,000-£60,000 bracket is subject to the child benefit charge if you are the highest earner in a household that receives child benefit.

In Chapter 19 we saw how pension contributions reduce your adjusted net income, which may help you reduce or completely avoid the child benefit charge.

Example

Archie normally has taxable income of £100,000. Just before the end of the current 2020/21 tax year he calculates that his taxable income has fallen to £65,000 this year, thanks to the economic shock caused by the coronavirus crisis. His wife earns £30,000 and receives child benefit for three children: £2,545.

On the top £15,000 slice of his income, Archie faces an £8,545 tax charge: £6,000 income tax and a £2,545 child benefit charge.

Because he has built up a big cash buffer over the years he can afford to make a £15,000 gross pension contribution this year.

Archie's pension contribution will attract £6,000 income tax relief and, by reducing his adjusted net income to £50,000, allows him to entirely avoid the £2,545 child benefit charge. The total tax relief is £8,545 or 57% of his gross pension contribution.

Protecting Your Personal Allowance

Once your income exceeds £100,000 your income tax personal allowance is gradually taken away. Once your income reaches £125,000 this year you will have no personal allowance at all.

Income in the £100,000-£125,000 bracket faces a hefty marginal income tax rate of 60%. However, as we saw in Chapter 20, pension contributions reduce your adjusted net income which means anyone in this income bracket who makes pension contributions can enjoy 60% tax relief.

If your taxable income is normally significantly higher than £125,000 but you expect it to fall back closer to £125,000 this year, you may be able to enjoy above average levels of tax relief on your pension contributions this year.

Example

Lana normally has taxable income of around £150,000 and therefore normally has all of her income tax personal allowance taken away. Just before the end of the current tax year she calculates that her taxable income has fallen to around £120,000 this year. With this much income she will lose £10,000 of her personal allowance.

Just before the end of the tax year she invests £16,000 in her pension. She receives a £4,000 top up from the taxman (her basic-rate tax relief), resulting in a gross pension contribution of £20,000. She will also receive higher-rate tax relief of £4,000 (£20,000 x 20%).

In addition, by making a gross pension contribution of £20,000 her adjusted net income will be reduced from £120,000 to £100,000, so none of her personal allowance will be taken away. Additional tax saving: £4,000 (£10,000 x 40%).

In summary, her £20,000 pension contribution produces £12,000 of tax savings – a total of 60% tax relief!

As we saw in Chapter 20, even if your income is more than £125,000 making quite big pension contributions can still be attractive because you may still get 60% tax relief on some of the money you put away.

For example, let's say your taxable income has fallen to £135,000 this year. If you invest £28,000 in a pension (a gross contribution of £35,000) you will enjoy £19,000 of tax savings – a total of 54% tax relief.

Anyone with taxable income up to £150,000 will enjoy *at least* 50% tax relief by making a gross pension contribution that's big enough to take their adjusted net income back down to £100,000.

Chapter 42

Future Changes to Pensions and Tax

As we all know, the Government has thrown a huge amount of money at supporting individuals and businesses during the coronavirus crisis.

This gigantic surge in spending will be financed through increased borrowing but eventually there will have to be a reckoning and this will probably mean higher taxes.

Any tax increases will probably target higher income earners and those with assets. We can expect politicians to start using that phrase "it's only fair that those with the broadest shoulders pay a little more," just as they did during the 2008 financial crisis.

Broader tax increases should also be expected. Chancellor Rishi Sunak has already stated that everyone will have to "chip in" to right the ship.

One possible target could be higher-rate tax relief on pension contributions.

Higher-rate Tax Relief on Pension Contributions

Higher-rate tax relief is estimated to cost the Government around £10 billion per year. For many years now commentators in the media and the pensions industry have been warning us that higher-rate tax relief will be taken away at some point. Higher-rate taxpayers have been encouraged to make bigger pension contributions while the relief is still available.

To date all such predictions have turned out to be hopelessly wrong. Sometimes I wonder if pension companies deliberately cry wolf about higher-rate tax relief in order to boost the amount of money they manage.

Most recently there were rumours that an announcement would be made in the March 2020 Budget by Sajid Javid, before he resigned as Chancellor of the Exchequer. There was no bad news from his replacement, current Chancellor Rishi Sunak.

In fact, Mr Sunak did the exact opposite. He raised the income threshold where the 'tapered annual allowance' kicks in from £150,000 to £240,000 (see Chapter 20). This change has made it possible for high income earners, for the first time in many years, to make pension contributions of up to £40,000 per year, just like everyone else. High income earners enjoy 45% tax relief on their pension contributions.

With the coronavirus bailouts wreaking havoc on the public finances, there are once again fresh rumours going around that the Government will eventually target higher-rate tax relief to help repair the damage.

Scrapping higher-rate tax relief altogether would take away most of the incentive to save into a pension, unless there is also a contribution from an employer.

For example, in Chapter 41 it was shown that if you only receive basic-rate tax relief on your contributions and pay basic-rate tax on the income you eventually withdraw, you will end up with just 6.25% more income than someone who saves in an ISA.

It's much worse if you end up as a higher-rate taxpayer when you retire, for example if you also have income from other sources such as rental property. In this case you will end up with 12.5% *less* income than someone who uses an ISA to save for retirement.

Clearly, basic-rate tax relief does not provide enough incentive to put money into a locked box for many years. If higher-rate tax relief is scrapped many individuals will stop using pensions to save for retirement.

One alternative would be to give everyone tax relief of, say, 30% instead of just 20%. Another more radical option would be to completely replace the current pension model with something similar to the Lifetime ISA. Everyone would receive a 25% Government bonus on their savings and all withdrawals in retirement would be tax free (see Part 3 for more on Lifetime ISAs).

However, possibly the easiest and most likely change is a reduction in the annual allowance from £40,000 to, say, £30,000 or £20,000.

The vast majority of higher-rate taxpayers do not want to make pension contributions anywhere close to £40,000 per year and so reducing the annual allowance would avoid the political damage that a wholesale scrapping of higher-rate tax relief would cause.

The truth is nobody knows what will happen to pension tax relief in the years ahead. Further changes seem likely at some point.

Other possible future tax increases that may be introduced to pay for the Government's coronavirus spending include:

Freezing the Higher-rate Threshold
The higher-rate threshold was £45,000 back in 2017/18 and has increased by more than the rate of inflation to £50,000 today. The Government could therefore argue that freezing the threshold for several years is justifiable.

Freezing tax thresholds is the easiest way for governments to increase taxes without telling anyone.

Increasing Dividend Tax Rates
Dividend tax rates were increased by 7.5% in 2016 to punish company owners who take most of their income as dividends and pay little or no national insurance.

There would be little sympathy from the wider public if shareholders were once again forced to pay more tax. We wouldn't be surprised to see tax rates increase by 2.5 percentage points at some point.

Scrapping the Dividend Allowance
The dividend allowance was reduced from £5,000 to £2,000 in 2018. It could be reduced to, say, £1,000 or scrapped altogether, although we don't think this is likely because of the increased administrative burden it would place on HMRC.

Increasing the Additional Rate
The additional rate was reduced from 50% to 45% in 2013. Increasing the rate back to 50% would be much easier than raising the 20% basic rate or 40% higher rate. The additional rate for dividend income is currently 38.1% and that could be raised too.

A Penny (or Two) on Income Tax
During the 2019 general election the Liberal Democrats pledged to increase all income tax rates by 1% to raise money for the NHS. They said this would raise £7 billion a year. Such a tax increase would be more politically palatable for a Conservative Government following the coronavirus pandemic.

Increasing National Insurance Rates
Salary earners, sole traders and business partners pay 2% national insurance on income over £50,000. This rate could be increased to help fund the NHS and to help fund other state benefits.

On income below £50,000 self-employed people currently pay 9% national insurance compared with the 12% paid by salary earners. We can expect the rate for self-employed business owners to be brought in line with those of salary earners. Chancellor Rishi Sunak has already hinted that this will happen.

Scrapping Entrepreneurs Relief
Entrepreneurs Relief allows you to pay just 10% capital gains tax when you sell your business or wind it up. In the March 2020 Budget the lifetime limit was reduced from £10 million of capital gains to just £1 million. We wouldn't rule out a further reduction or even a complete scrapping of this tax relief.

Increasing Capital Gains Tax
We also wouldn't rule out wider increases in capital gains tax because people with assets are an easy political target. At present higher-rate taxpayers pay 28% capital gains tax when they sell residential property and 20% when they sell other assets. These rates could be increased fairly significantly at the stroke of a pen.

Inheritance Tax
Changes to inheritance tax have been widely mooted following a report by the Orwellian Office of Tax Simplification. However, no changes were made in the March 2020 Budget.

The inheritance tax nil rate band has been frozen at its current level of £325,000 since 6 April 2009. In the absence of a major overhaul of the grave robbers tax, the £325,000 exemption could remain frozen for many more years. And because people with significant assets are such an easy political target, it would be fairly easy to introduce a tax rate higher than the current 40% for larger estates.

Stamp Duty Land Tax
Because people who buy expensive assets are such an easy political target, we wouldn't rule out increases in the stamp duty land tax payable on expensive properties.

VAT
The Government has frozen the VAT registration threshold at £85,000 until 31st March 2022.

The Office of Tax Simplification would like to see a drastic reduction in the threshold on the grounds that a high threshold limits the amount of work small businesses take on.

In the absence of any big changes it would be fairly easy to keep the current threshold at £85,000 for several more years to gradually drag more businesses into the tax net.

A Final Word on Potential Tax Increases
It's important to stress that all of the above is highly speculative. We do not know what tax changes policymakers have up their sleeves but we wouldn't be at all surprised if at least some of these measures are introduced in the years ahead.

We're also not making any moral judgements about whether any such tax increases would be right or wrong. The country's finances will be in a mess when we get through the coronavirus pandemic, as will the finances of many taxpayers who may wish to do what they can to protect their families.

Chapter 43

ISAs, VCTs and Mortgages

Introduction

Some investments are much more liquid than others, meaning you can get your hands on your money quickly if you need it.

We've already discussed in Chapter 41 why it may be a good idea to reduce or halt your pension contributions this year if you are worried about your finances. This is because pension savings are placed in a locked box until you're 55 and there are other restrictions when you start withdrawing money.

The general rule is the more generous the tax shelter, the more difficult it is to get your hands on your money. So this year many individuals may have to consider sacrificing tax savings in favour of retaining access to their cash.

Traditional ISAs

Instant access cash ISAs are arguably the most liquid type of tax shelter because you can generally get hold of your money at any time.

Some cash ISAs do, however, have a 120 day notice period and don't offer much more interest than instant access accounts.

Fixed-rate ISAs offer a fixed rate for between one and five years and there will be a penalty if you withdraw any money before the end of the term.

The investments in a stocks and shares ISA can be liquidated at any time and the cash can be paid out, although this may not be very appealing if your investments are all showing a loss at present!

Lifetime ISAs

Those aged 18 to 39 can open a Lifetime ISA which can be used to save for a first home or for retirement.

Any money you put in (up to £4,000 per year) receives a 25% Government bonus. So if you put in £4,000, the Government will add £1,000.

See Part 3 of this guide for full details.

Unlike a pension, your savings are not locked up inside a Lifetime ISA and can be accessed in a financial emergency.

If you withdraw money before reaching age 60, for any reason other than to buy your first home, there will normally be a 25% early withdrawal charge. This will claw back all of the Government bonus, plus an additional 6.25% of the amount you invested.

For example, if you invest £1,000, the Government will add £250, giving you total savings of £1,250. If you then decide to withdraw the money, the 25% penalty would be £312.50, leaving you with £937.50.

Thus early withdrawals will normally result in you losing the Government bonus plus an extra £62.50 (6.25%) out of the amount you originally invested.

This is what happens *normally*.

However, the Government has announced that the early withdrawal charge has been reduced temporarily from 25% to 20% for withdrawals taking place between 6 March and 5 April 2021.

This is to help those currently experiencing financial difficulty. It means early withdrawals from a Lifetime ISA will result in the Government bonus being taken away but will not result in any additional penalty for now.

This announcement means that a Lifetime ISA is a relatively attractive savings vehicle in the current economic environment.

Junior ISAs

Junior ISAs are available for minors. Parents, grandparents and others can invest up to £9,000 this year, a big increase over last year.

However, no withdrawals are permitted before the child is 18 years old. For this reason grandparents, in particular, should think twice about tying up money in these accounts. It may be better to hold onto the cash in case the parents need it in the months ahead and make catch-up contributions later on.

Junior SIPPS

Junior SIPPs were discussed in Chapter 39.

While they are a great way to build a long-term nest egg for your children or grandchildren, the money could be locked up for up to 60 years!

Just like Junior ISAs, grandparents in particular should think twice about tying up money in these accounts in the current climate.

It may be better to hold onto the cash in case the parents need it in the months ahead and make catch-up contributions later on.

Venture Capital Trusts

VCTs are generous tax shelters, providing 30% up front income tax relief and tax-free dividends and capital gains.

However, your money is effectively locked away for at least five years. So VCTs are not the best investment in the current climate for anyone worried about their personal cash position.

The share prices of some VCTs fell by over 50% during the coronavirus-led plunge in the stock market. This shows just how risky these investments can be.

Some may argue that now would be a good time for the brave to invest but you can also invest in ordinary small company funds via an ISA. You'll lose out on the 30% up front tax relief but your money will not be tied up.

Reducing Your Mortgage

Paying down your mortgage can be very tax efficient.

This is because not paying interest on the money you borrow is almost always much better than earning interest on the money you save.

If paying off £10,000 of debt means you don't have to pay 3% interest on that debt, you have effectively earned 3% tax free. That's much better than earning, say, 1% from a savings account.

However, reducing your mortgage in the current climate may not be a very good idea if it means you will no longer be able to get your hands on the cash you use to repay your mortgage.

It may be better to accept a smaller return by keeping your money in a savings account.